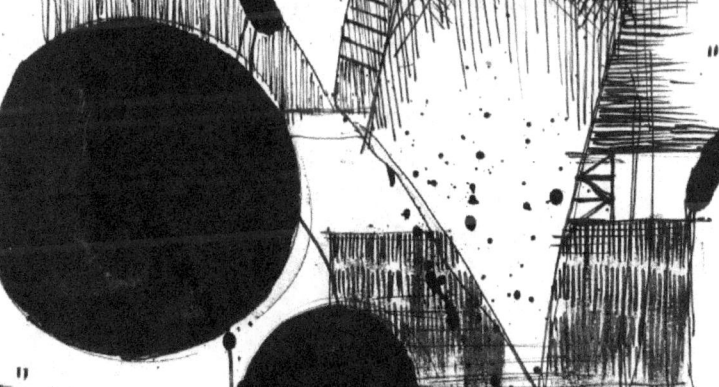

THE MONOCHROME COLLECTION VOL.1

FROM SKETCHBOOKS 1, 2 & 3

DANA KRYSTLE

Copyright © 2020 by Dana Krystle

Cover & Book Design by Dana Krystle

All rights reserved. No part of this book may be reproduced, transmitted, or stored in an information retrieval system in any form or by any means, graphic, electronic, or mechanical, including photocopying, taping, and recording, without prior written permission from the author.

ISBN: 9798559979007

Email: danakhalifa@live.com
Website: www.dana-krystle.com

Social Media :
Twitter : @dana_krystle
Instagram : @dana_krystle
Youtube : C/danakrystle

The Monochrome Collection Vol.1
from Sketchbooks 1, 2 & 3

By Dana Krystle

ABOUT THE AUTHOR

Born in 1989, an Architectural Designer, Artist and Author with a passion for experimental approaches & techniques. A German Jordanian University Graduate with multiple experiences in the field of Landscape Architecture, Heritage Conservation, Exhibition Design and Architecture Design. Her style was defined as Contemporary, Abstract and Uncanny. You will find her work posted in multiple websites showcasing her Architectural designs, Abstract Paintings, Travel Photography and the occasional Poetry excerpts which she publishes a -collection of- on a yearly basis.

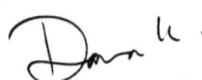

INTRODUCTION

The Monochrome Collection Vol.1 from Sketchbooks 1, 2 & 3 is part of a large sketchbook series in architecture illustrations created between 2013 and 2020, in this sketchbook the illustrations were created between 2017 and 2020. Materials used in this sketchbook are pen and ink. The aim of architecture illustrations are directed at creating inspiration and conceptual ideas that are used for creative concept decisions in projects and mood boards. I hope this sketchbook gives you inspiration for creating your own version of architecture illustration sketchbooks and even come up with beautiful architecture designs and concepts in your projects. A thorough documentation is set to collect and archive all the sketches that were created during this series and body of work.

Dana Krystle

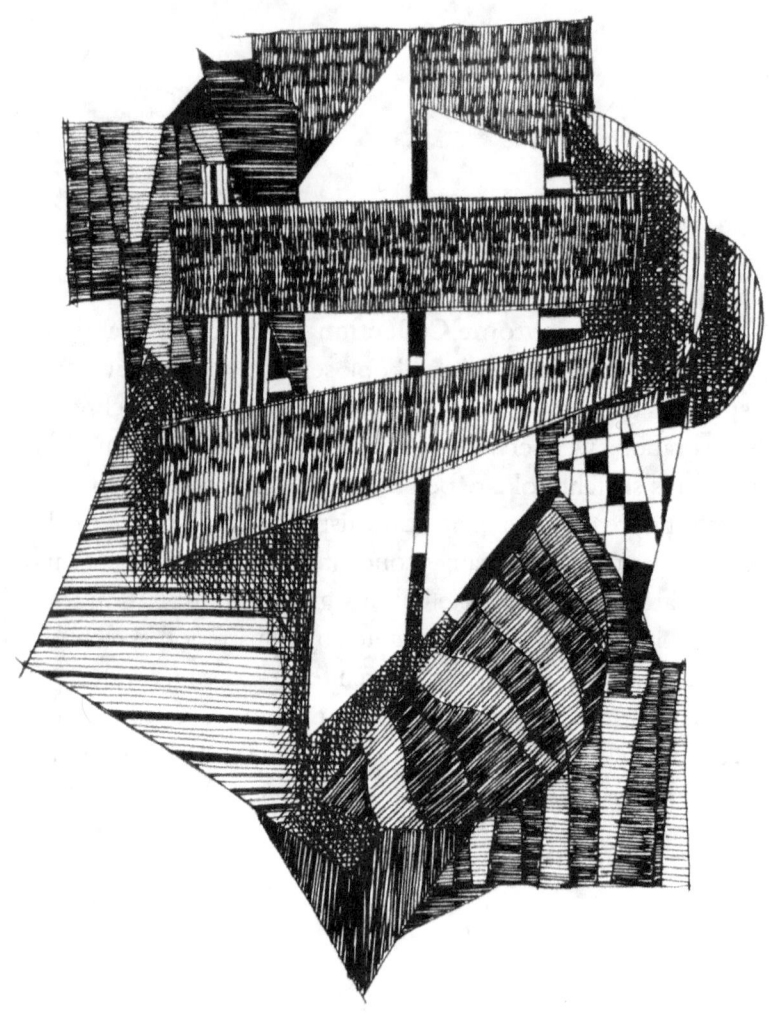

The Monochrome Collection Vol.1

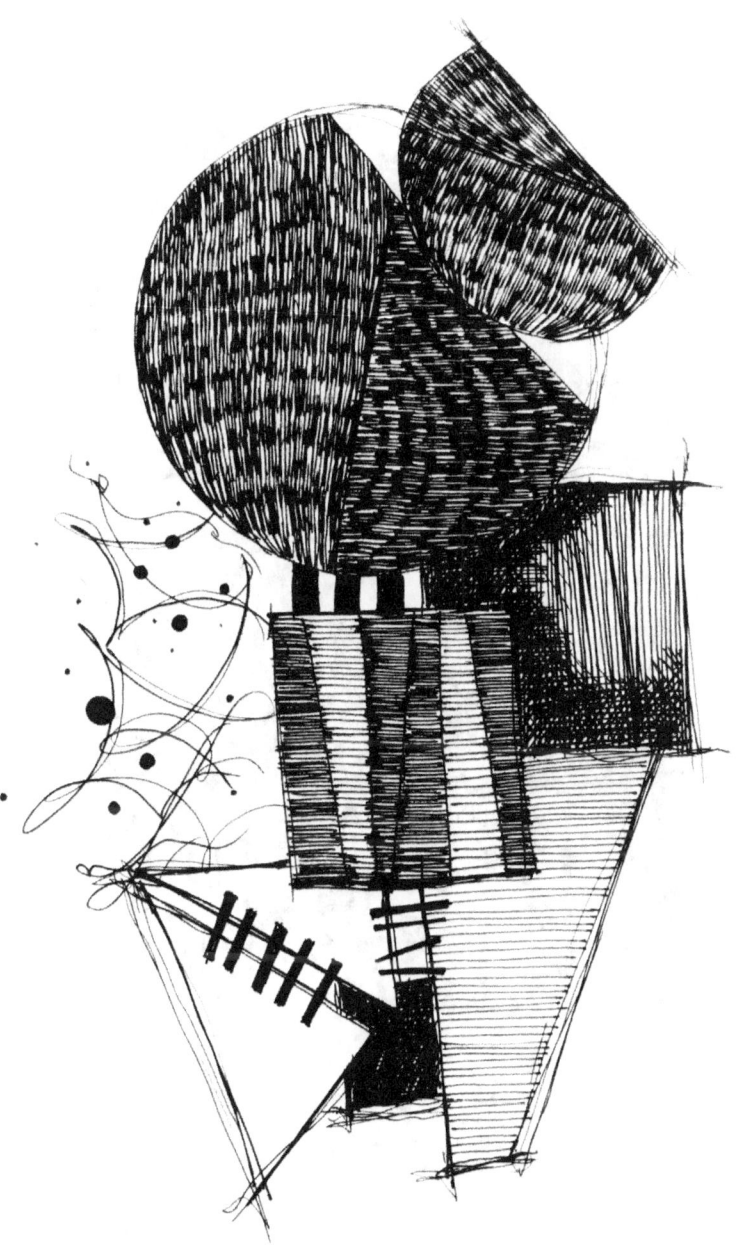

Dana Krystle

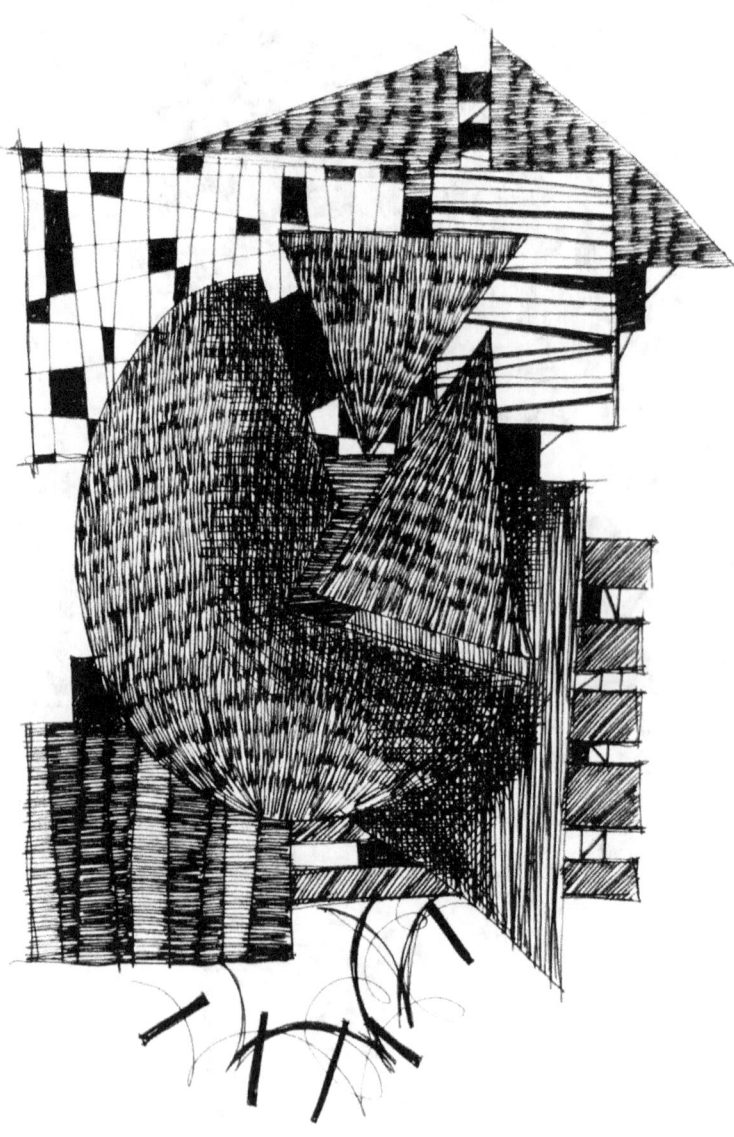

The Monochrome Collection Vol.1

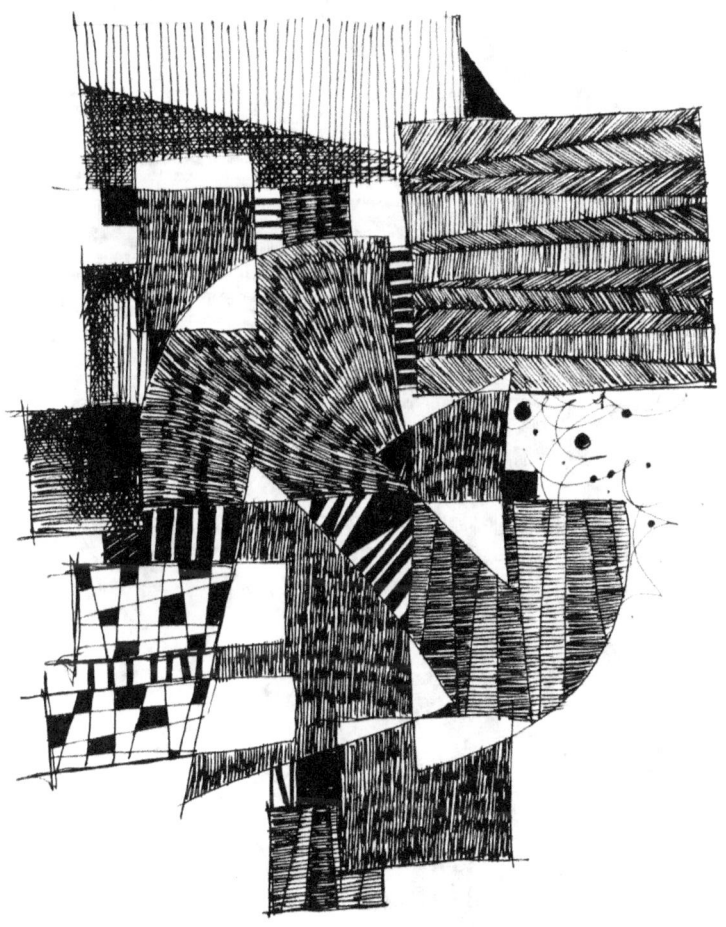

Dana Krystle

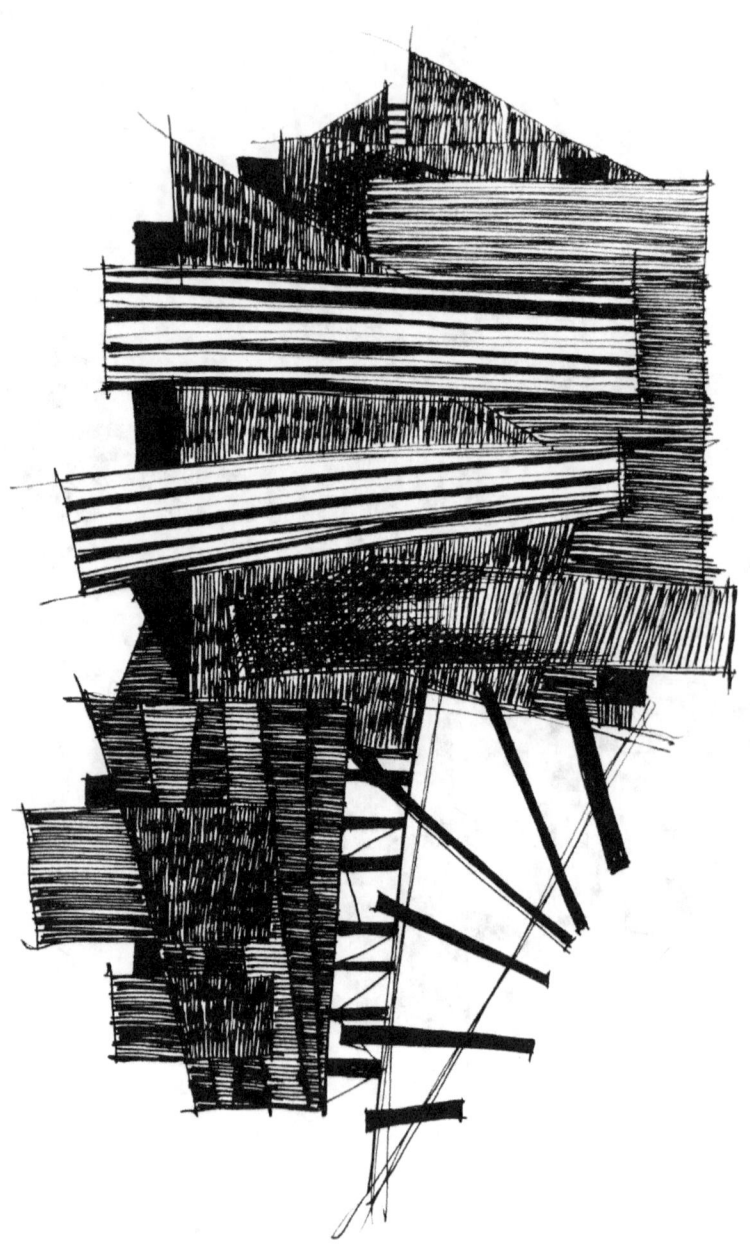

The Monochrome Collection Vol.1

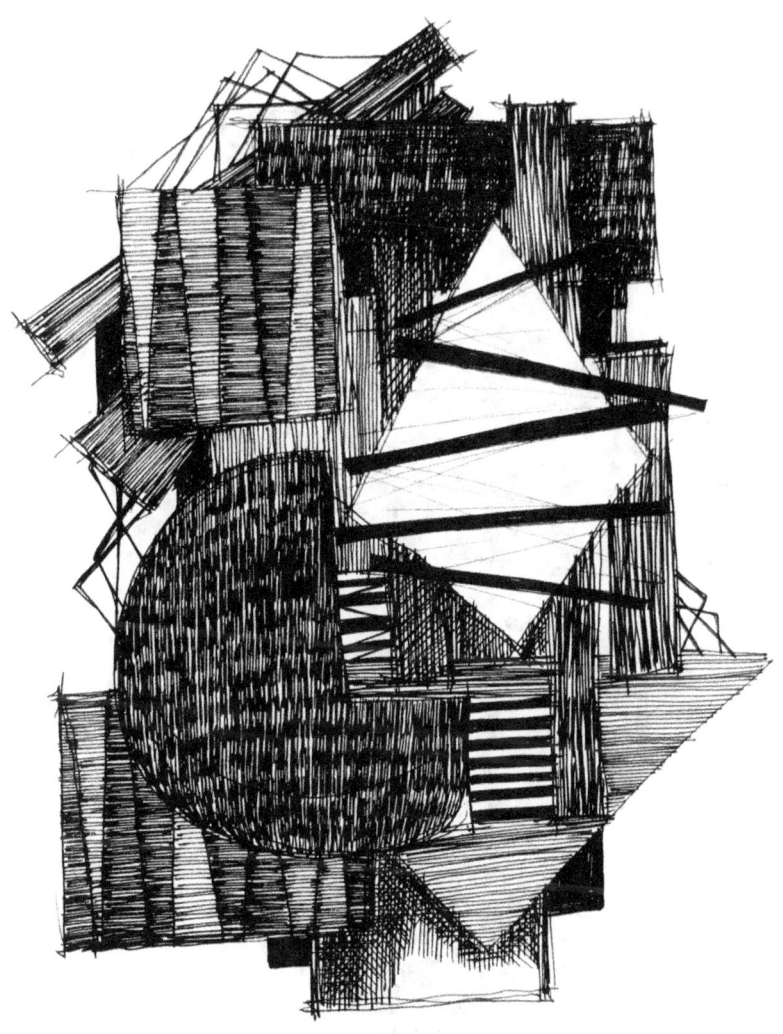

Dana Krystle

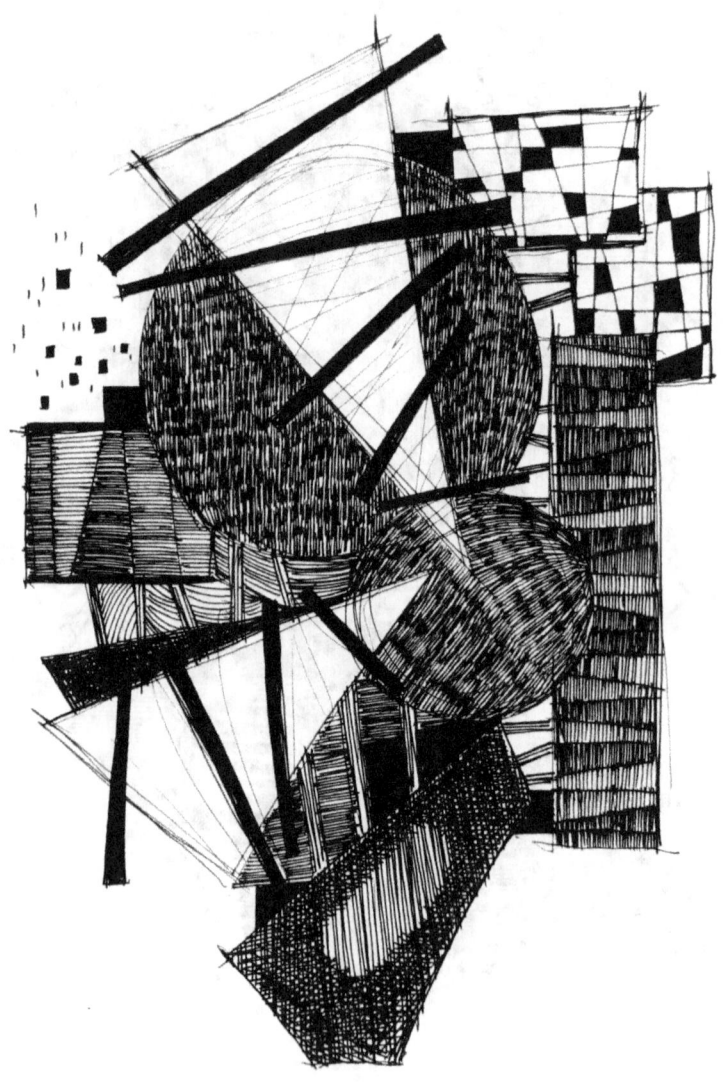

The Monochrome Collection Vol.1

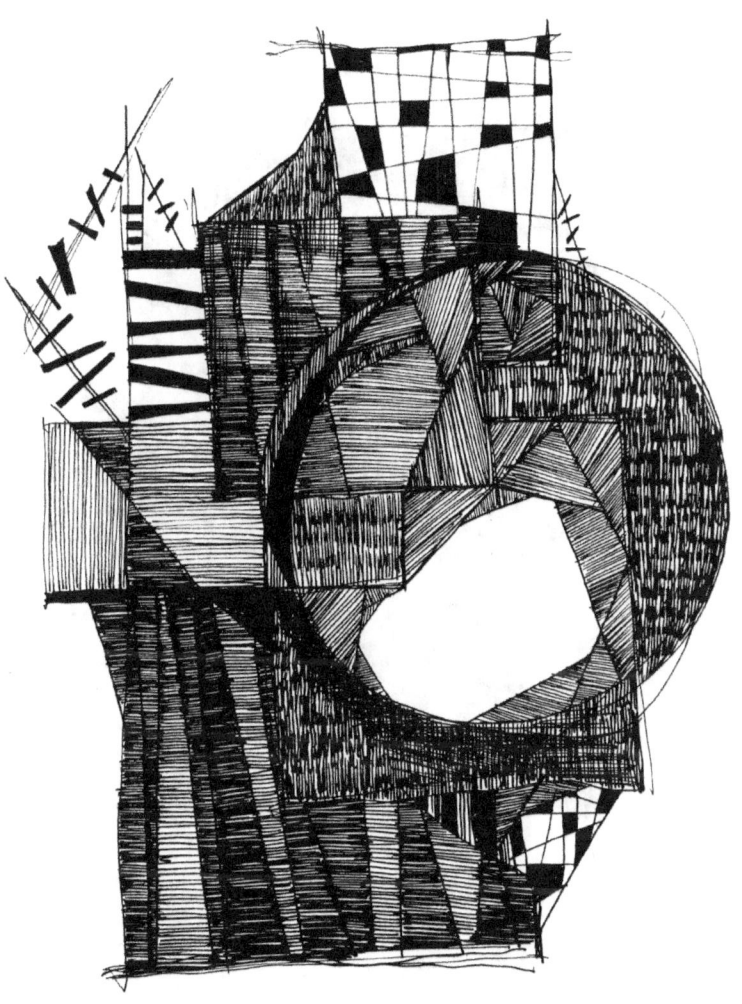

Dana Krystle

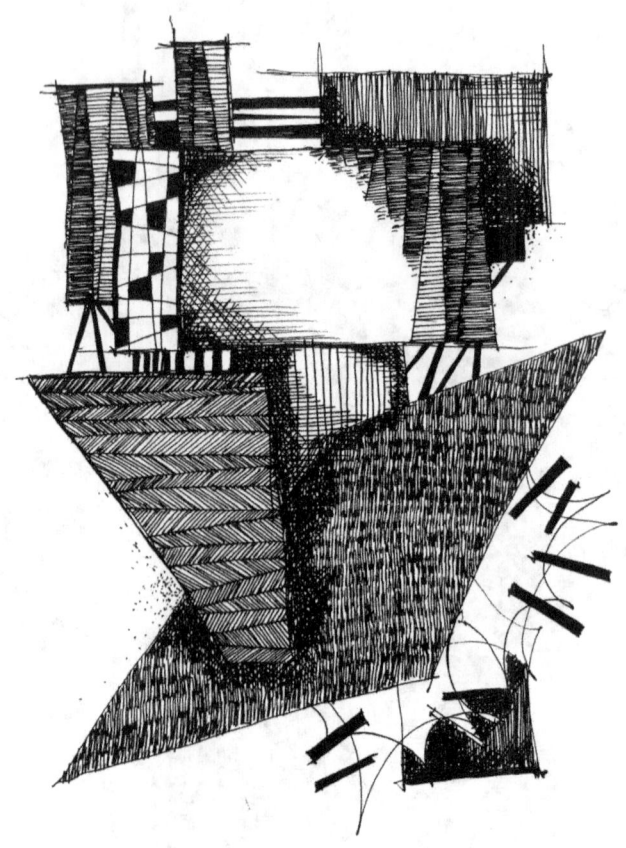

The Monochrome Collection Vol.1

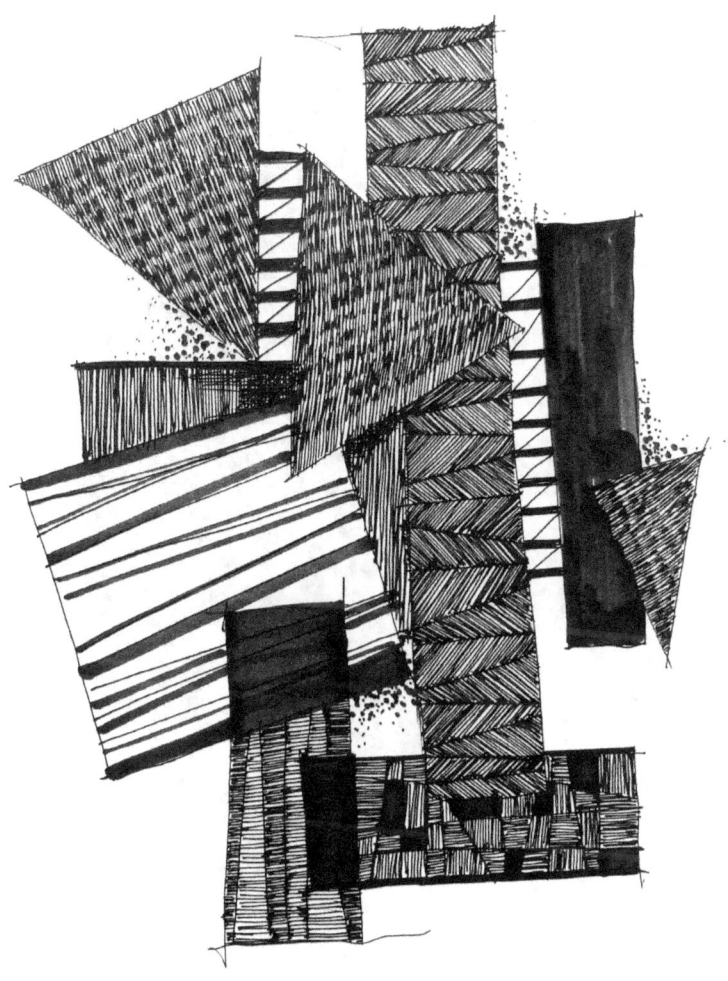

Dana Krystle

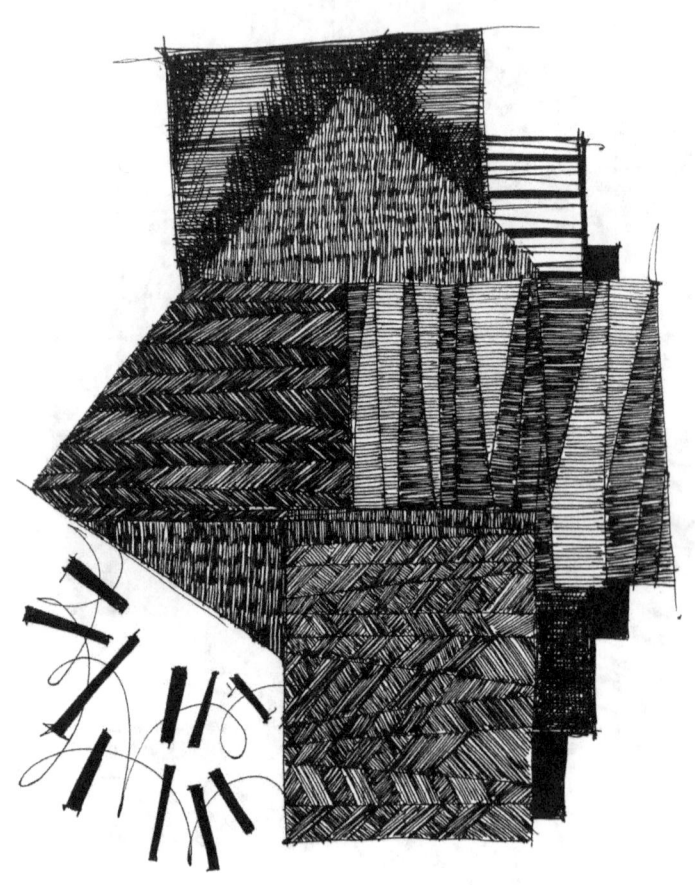

The Monochrome Collection Vol.1

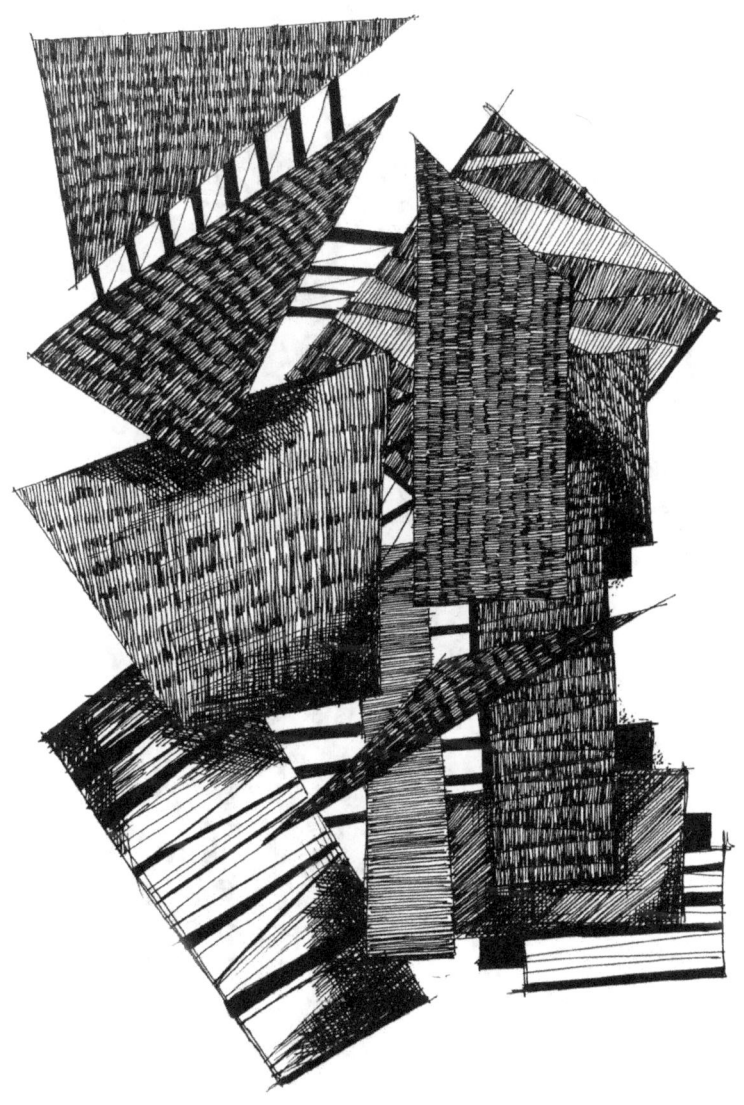

Dana Krystle

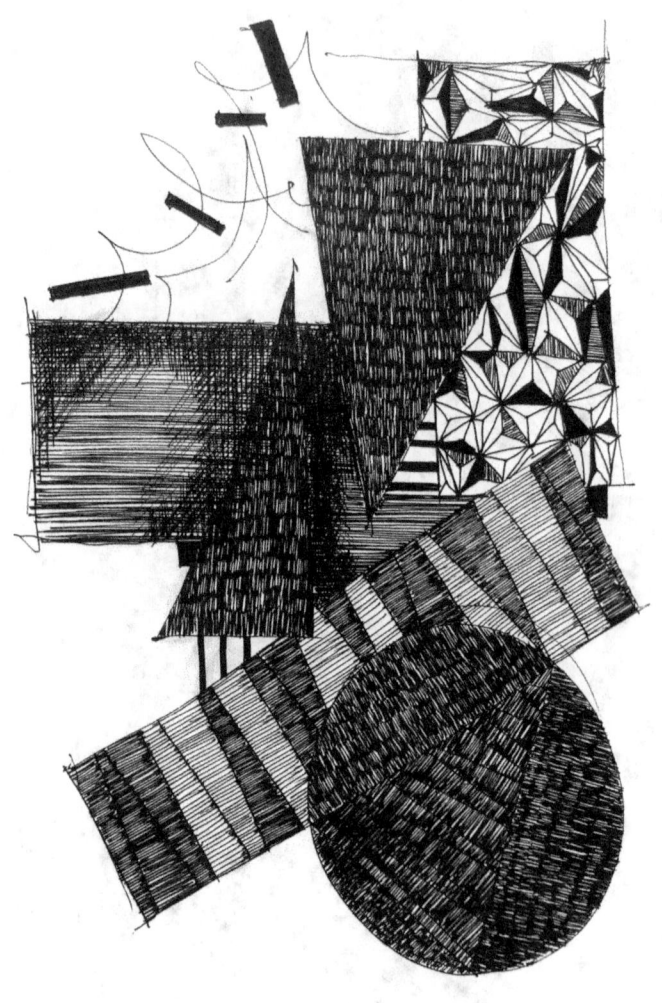

The Monochrome Collection Vol.1

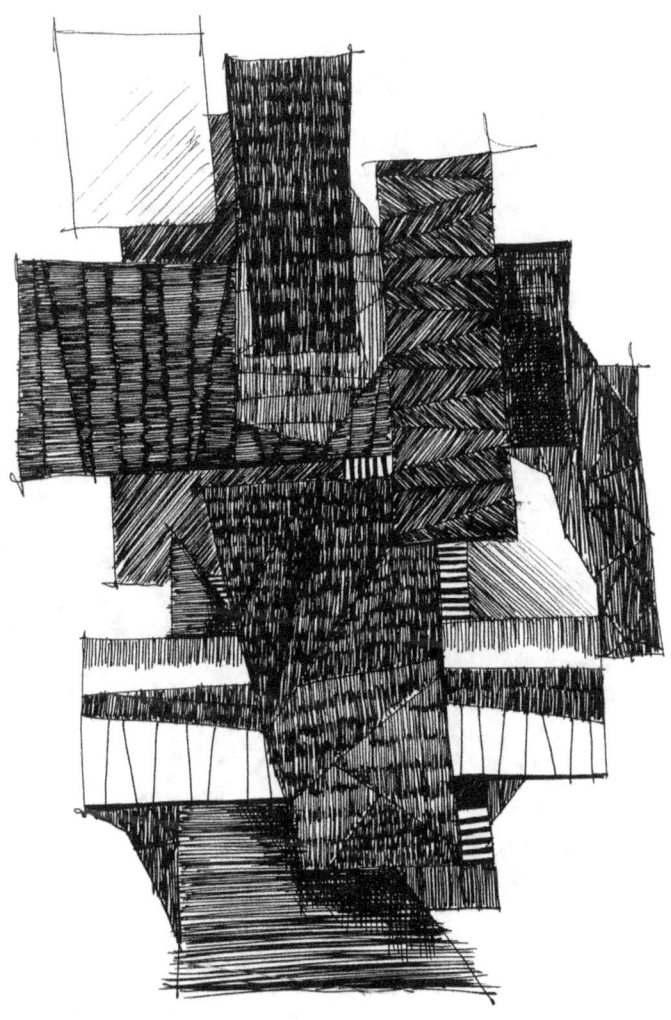

Dana Krystle

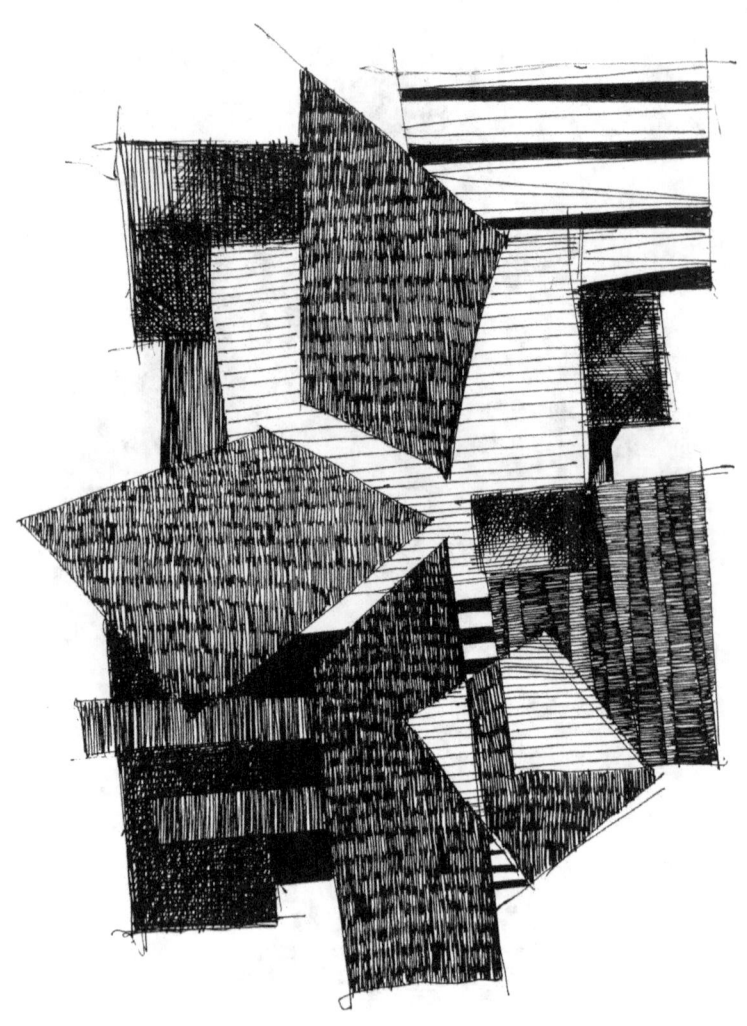

The Monochrome Collection Vol.1

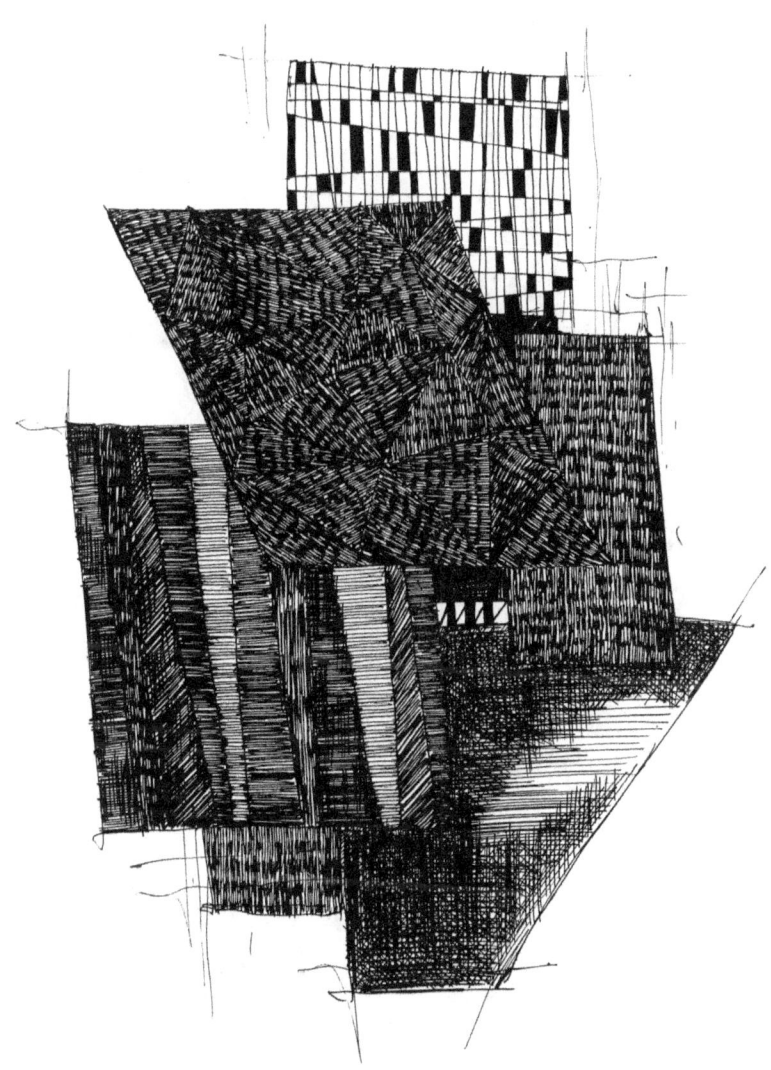

Dana Krystle

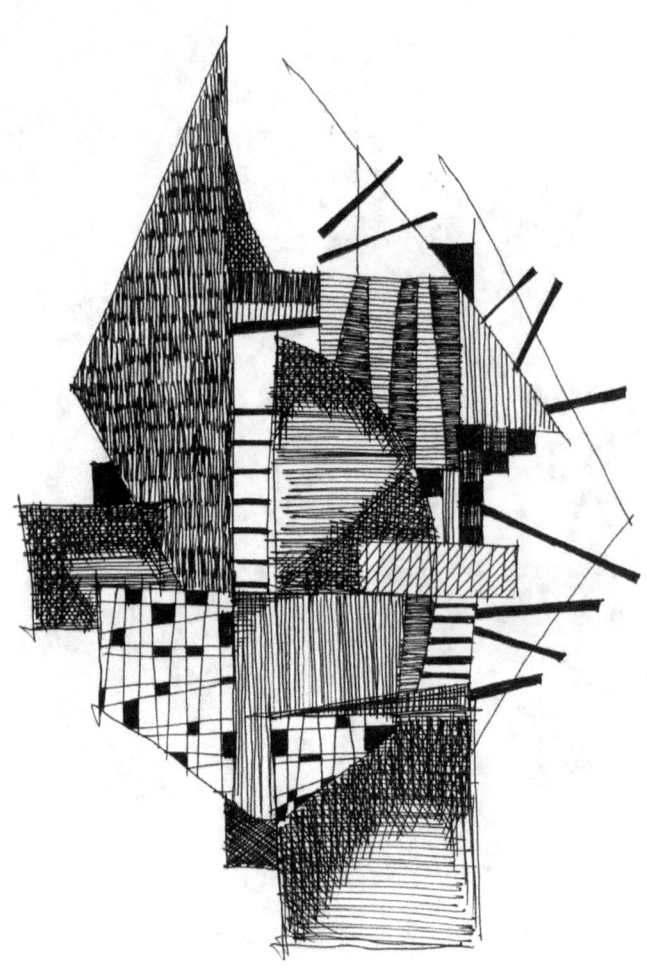

The Monochrome Collection Vol.1

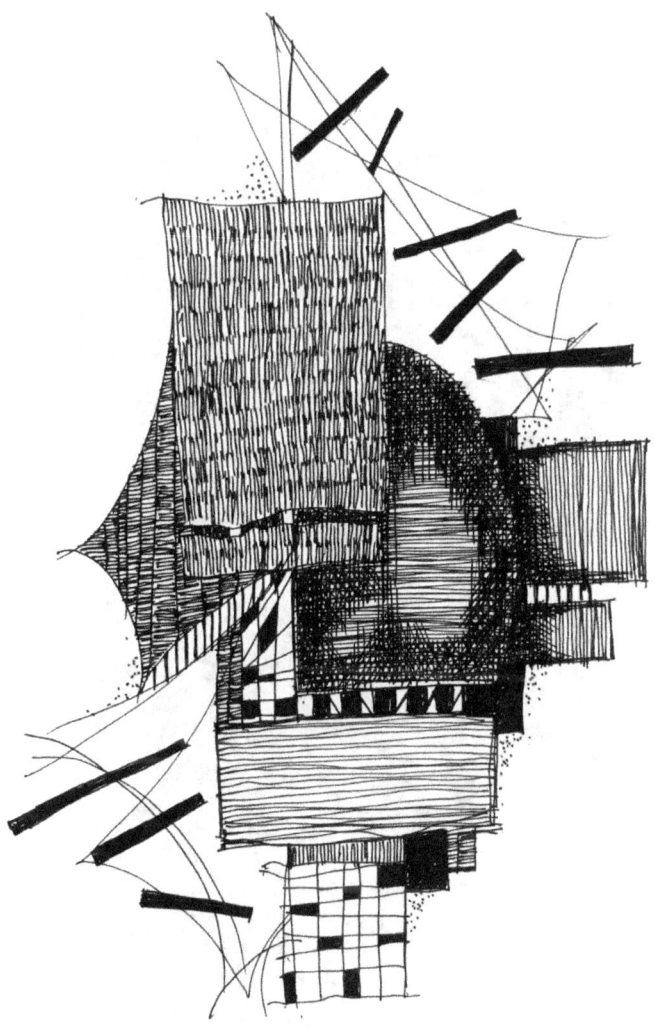

Dana Krystle

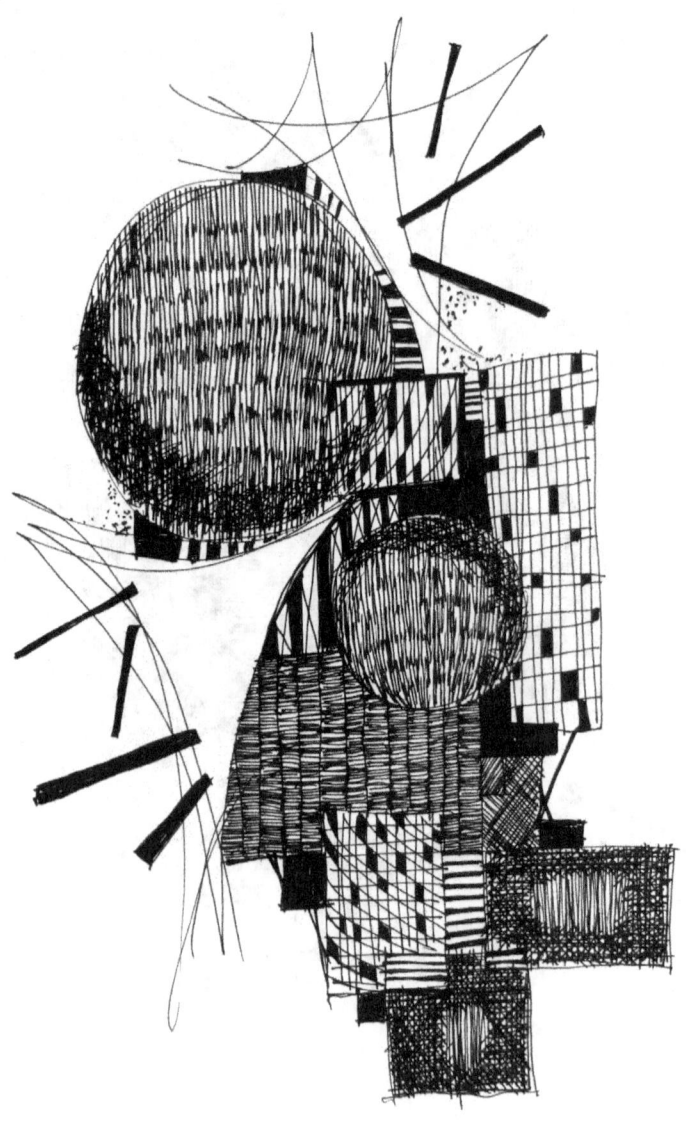

The Monochrome Collection Vol.1

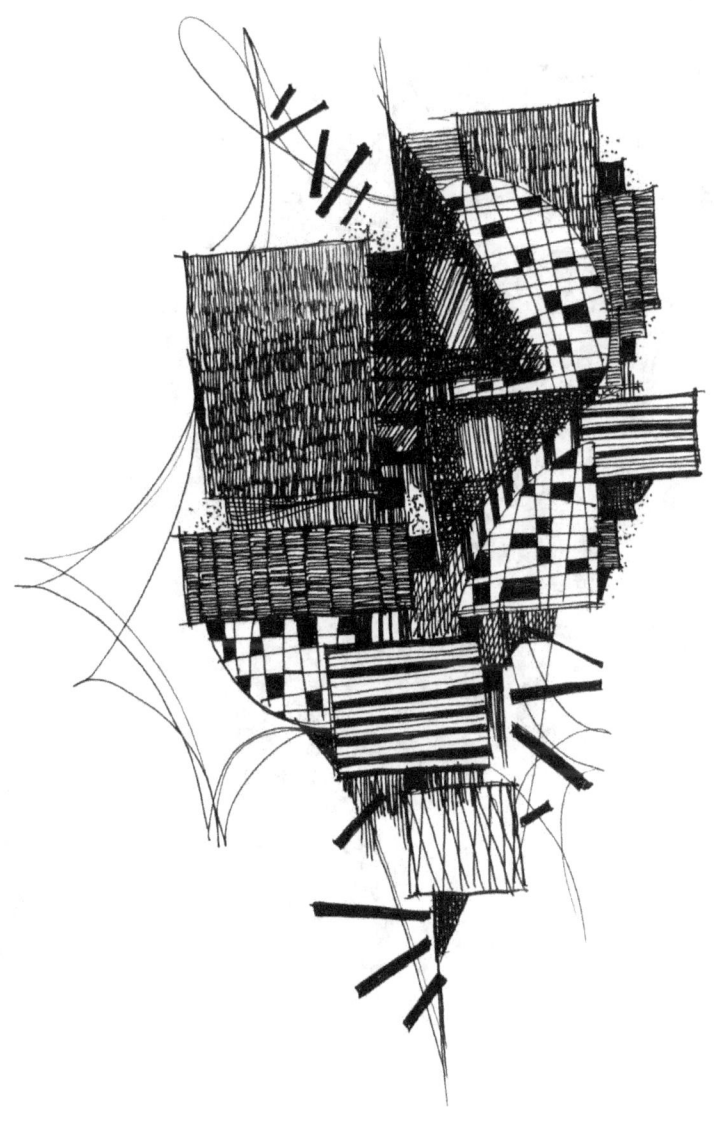

Dana Krystle

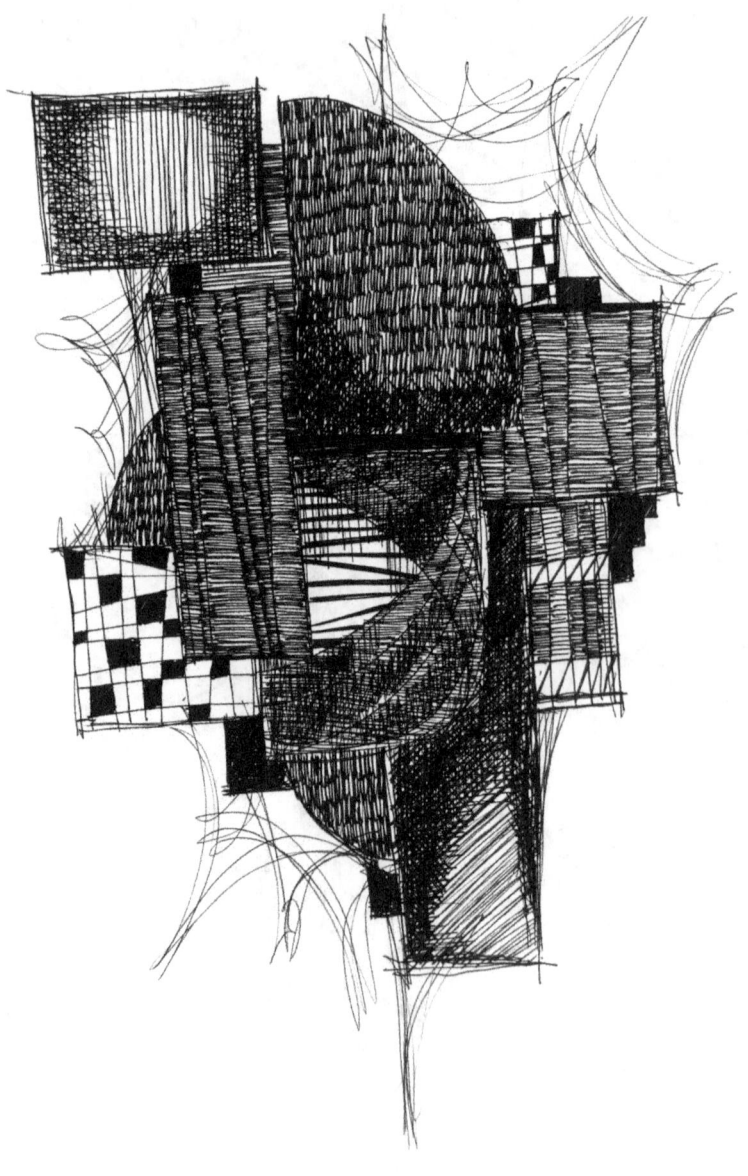

The Monochrome Collection Vol.1

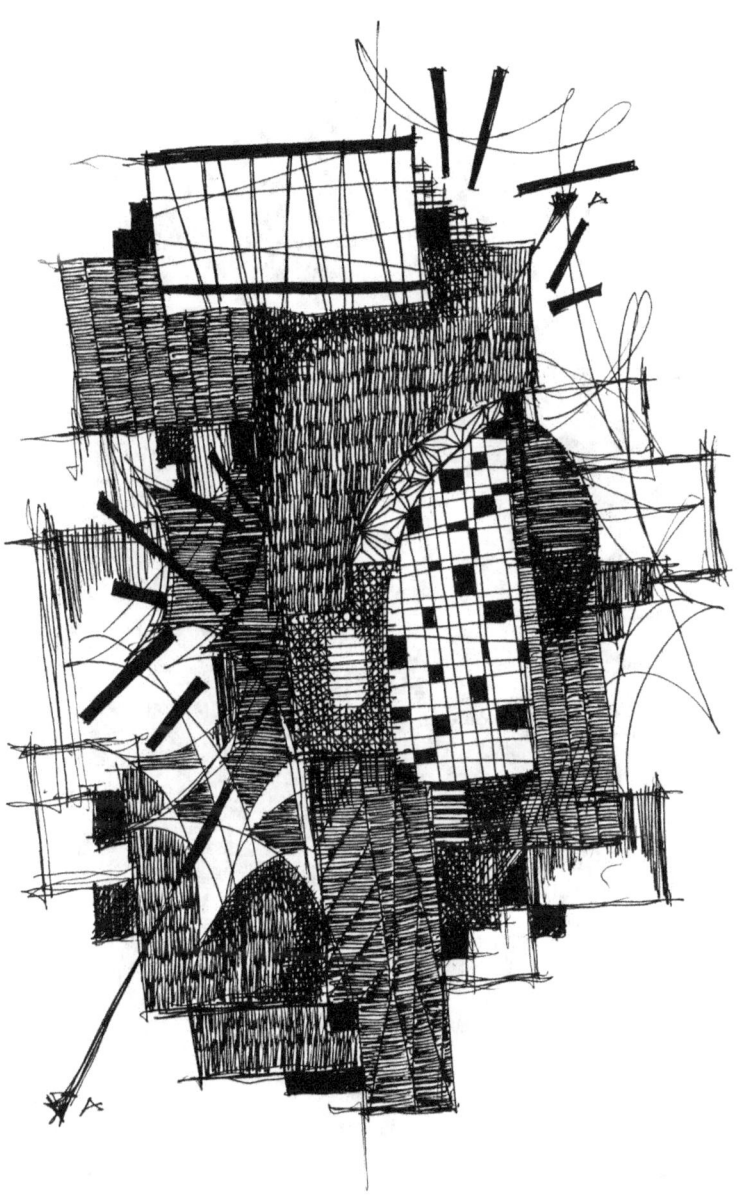

Dana Krystle

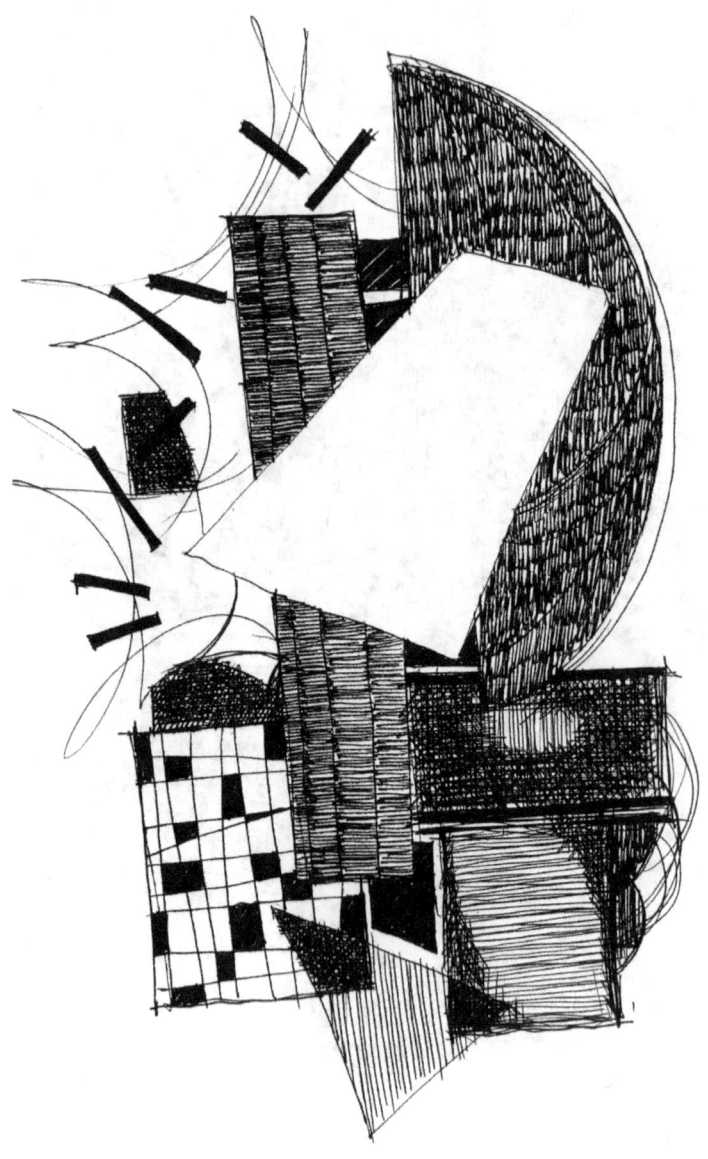

The Monochrome Collection Vol.1

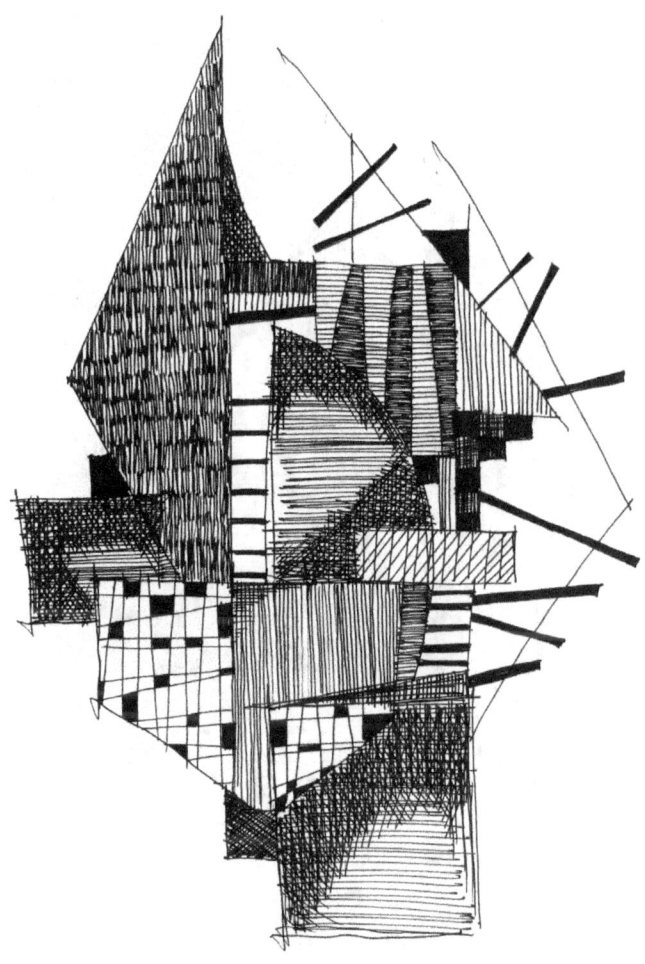

Dana Krystle

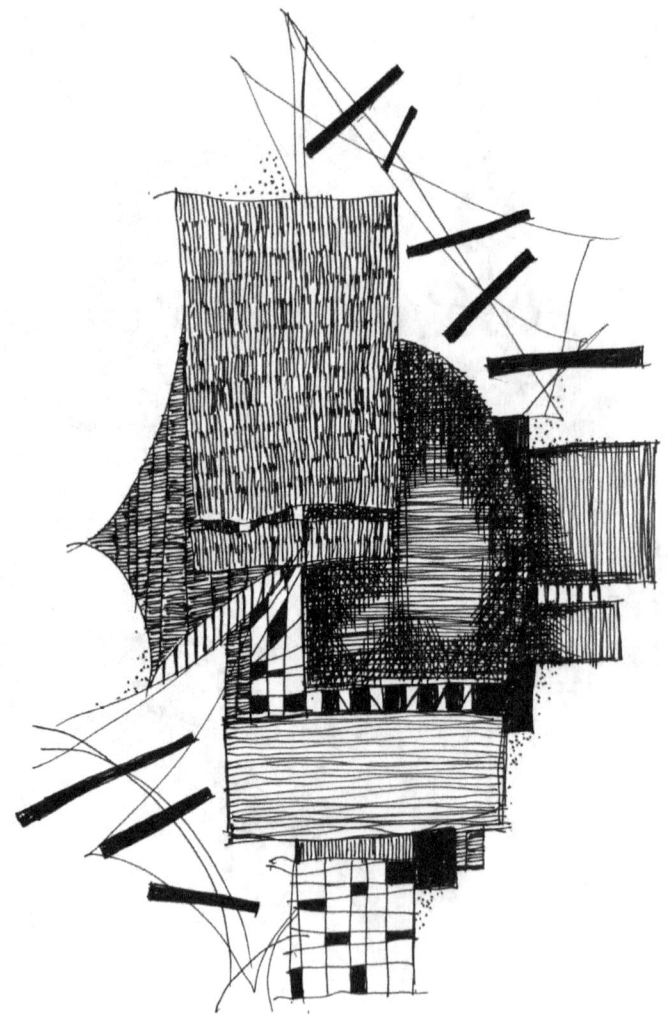

The Monochrome Collection Vol.1

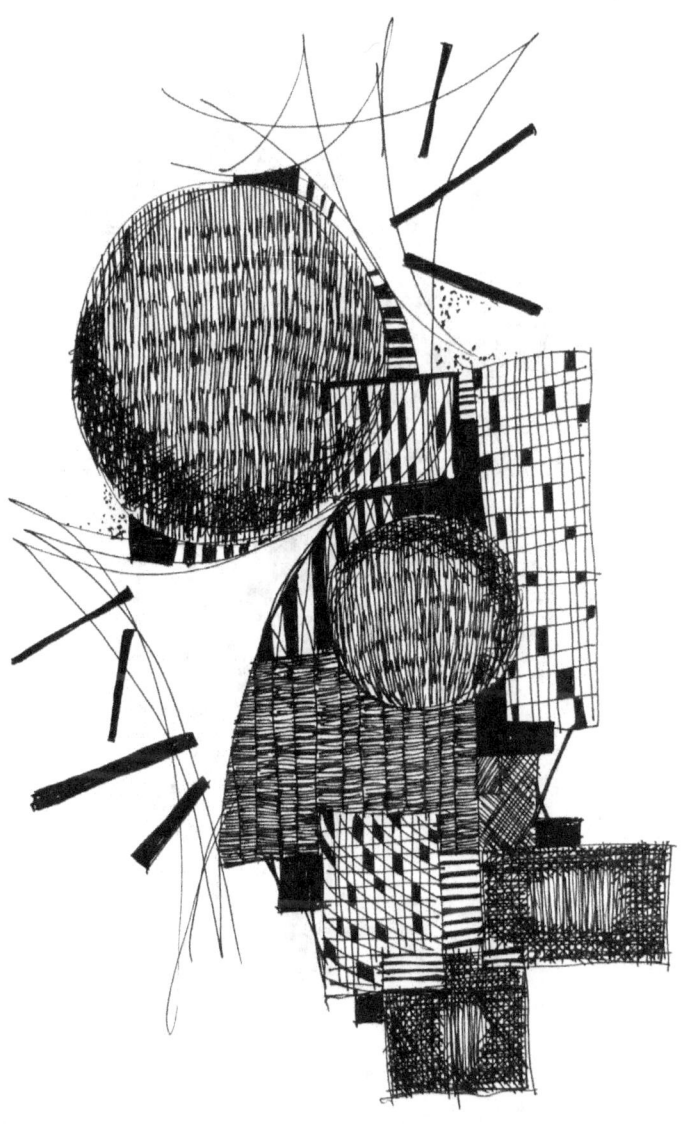

Dana Krystle

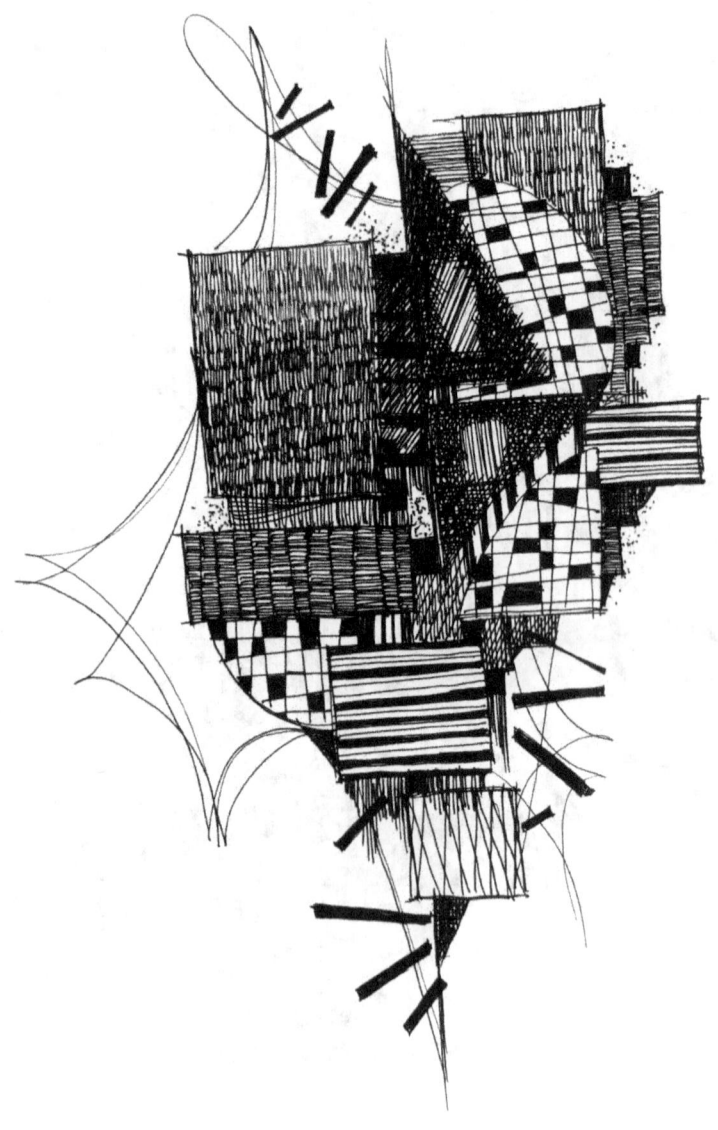

The Monochrome Collection Vol.1

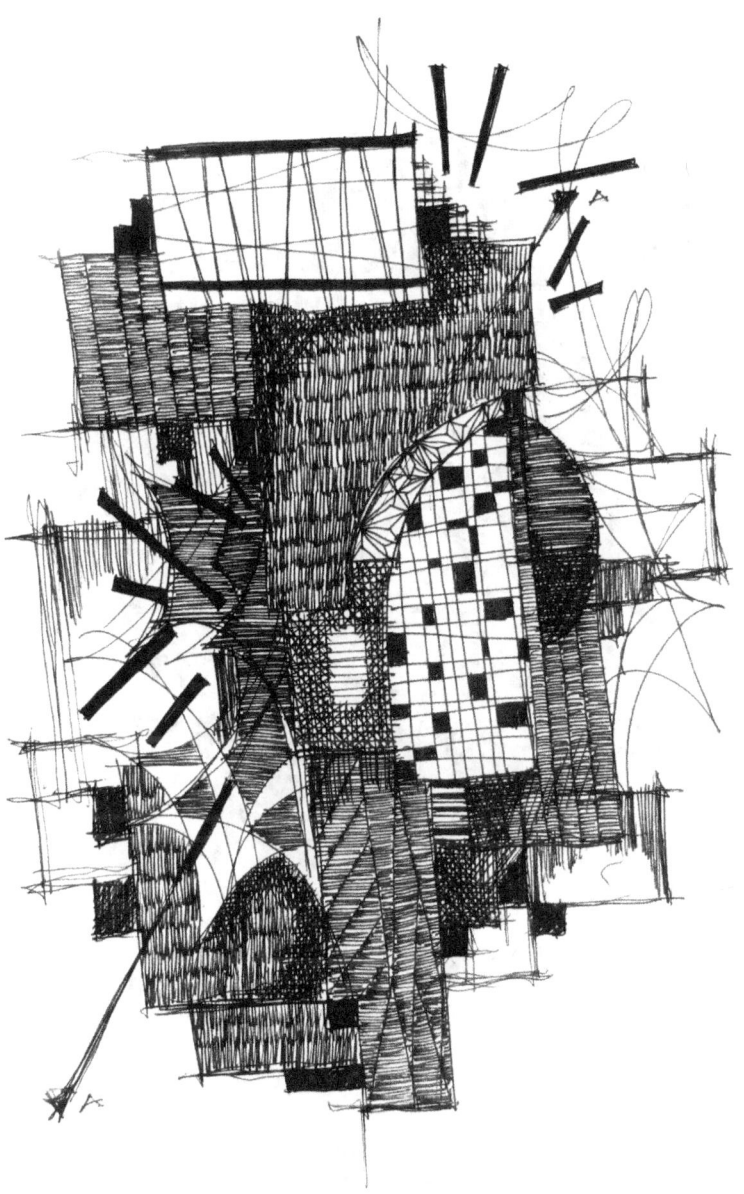

Dana Krystle

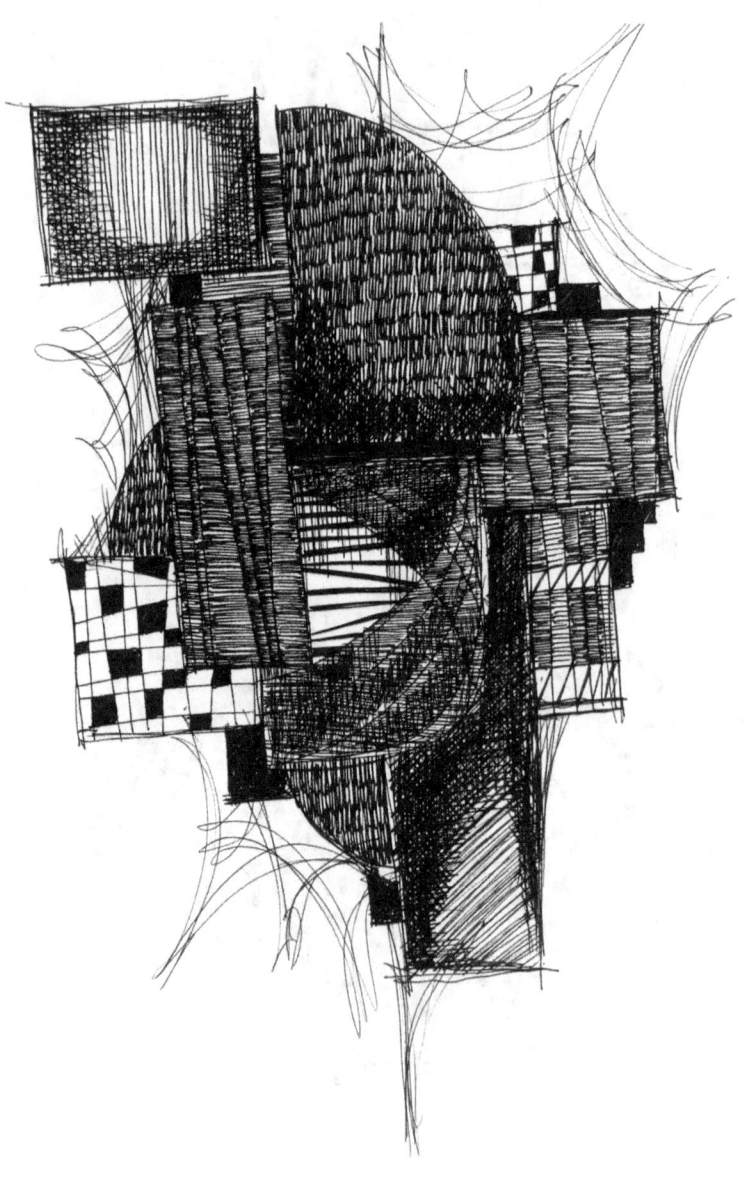

The Monochrome Collection Vol.1

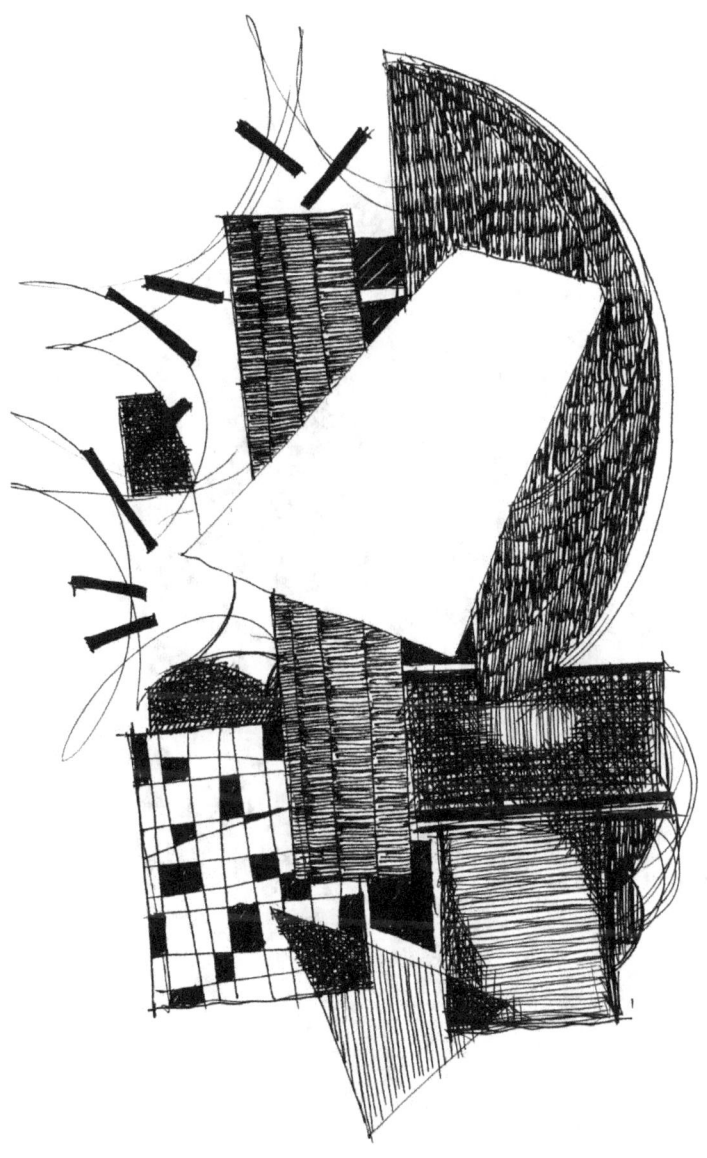

Dana Krystle

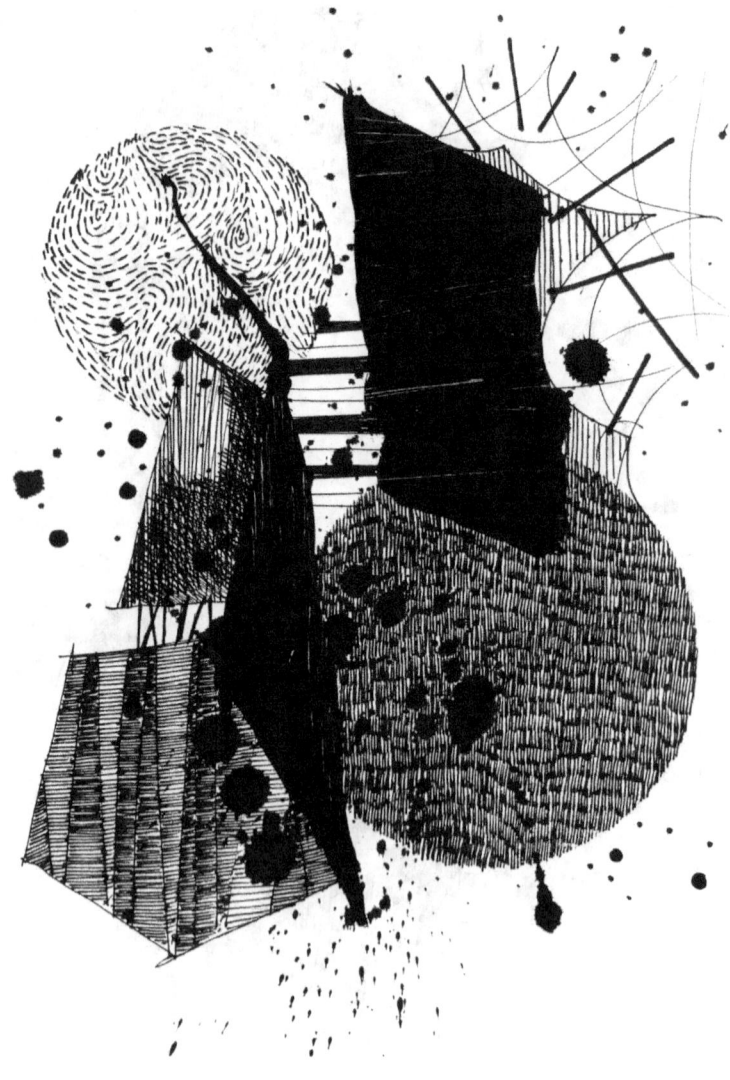

The Monochrome Collection Vol.1

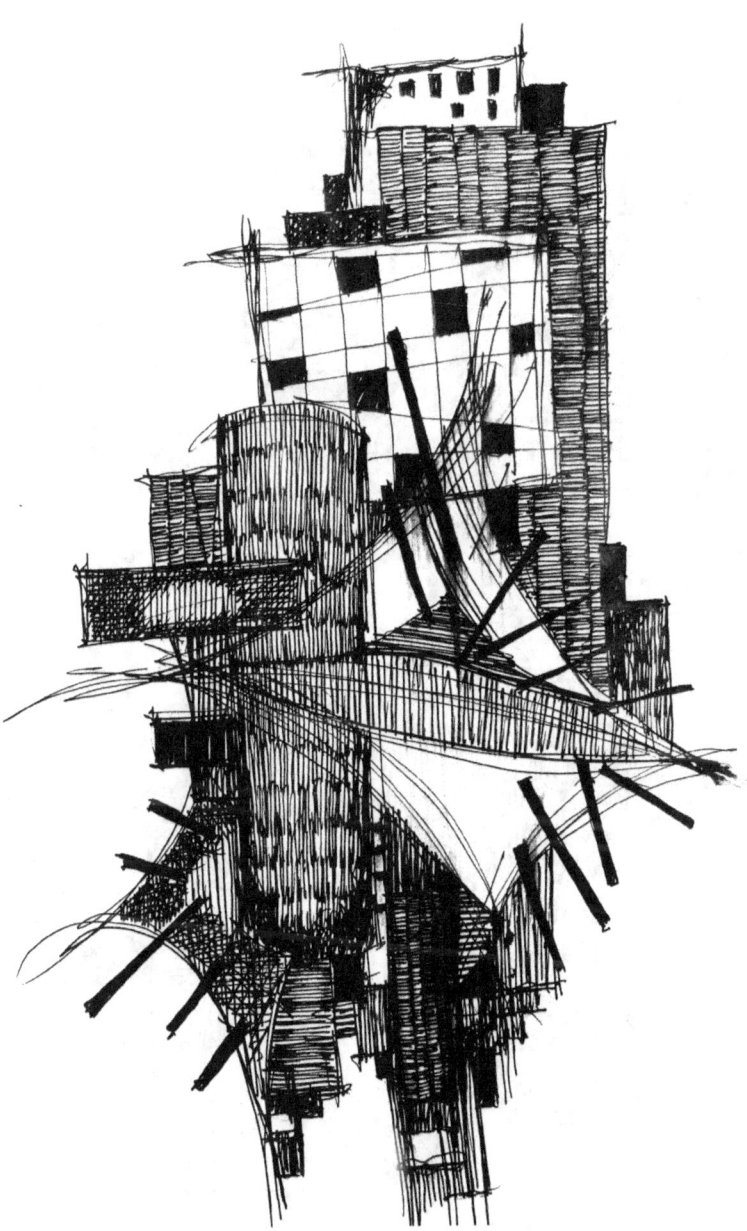

Dana Krystle

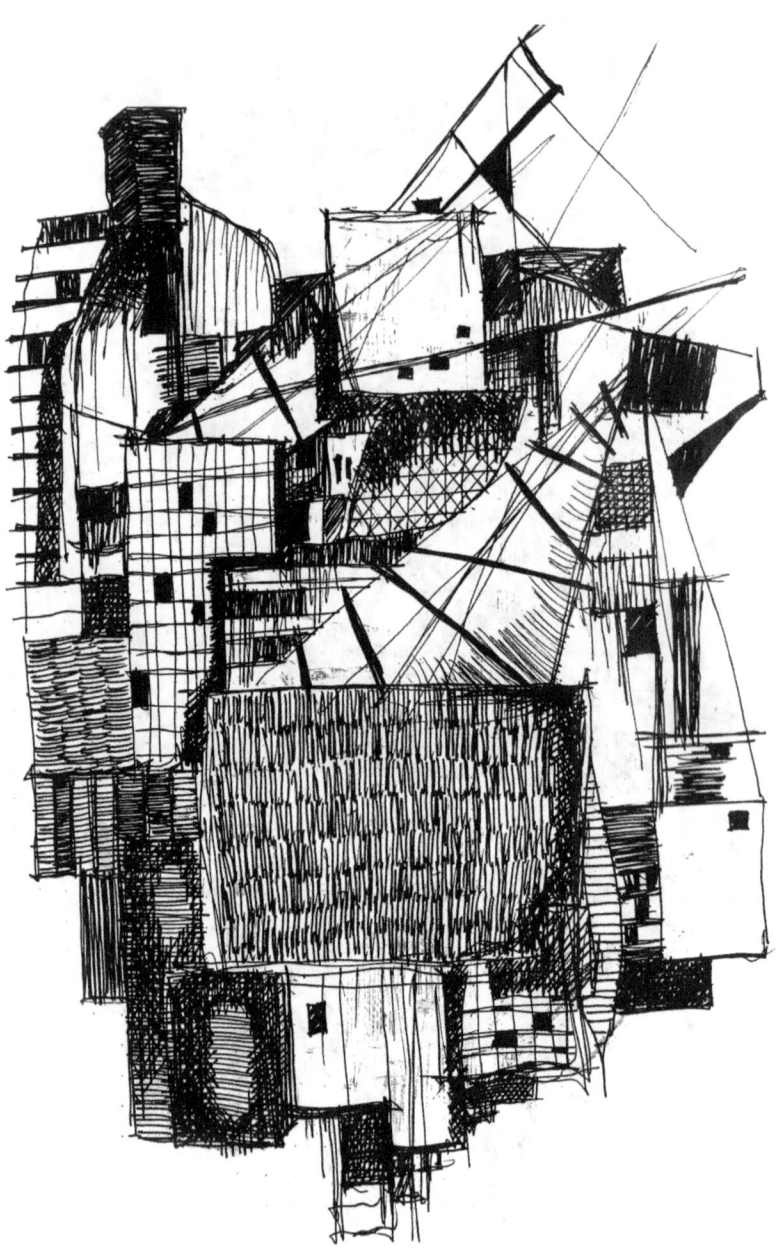

The Monochrome Collection Vol.1

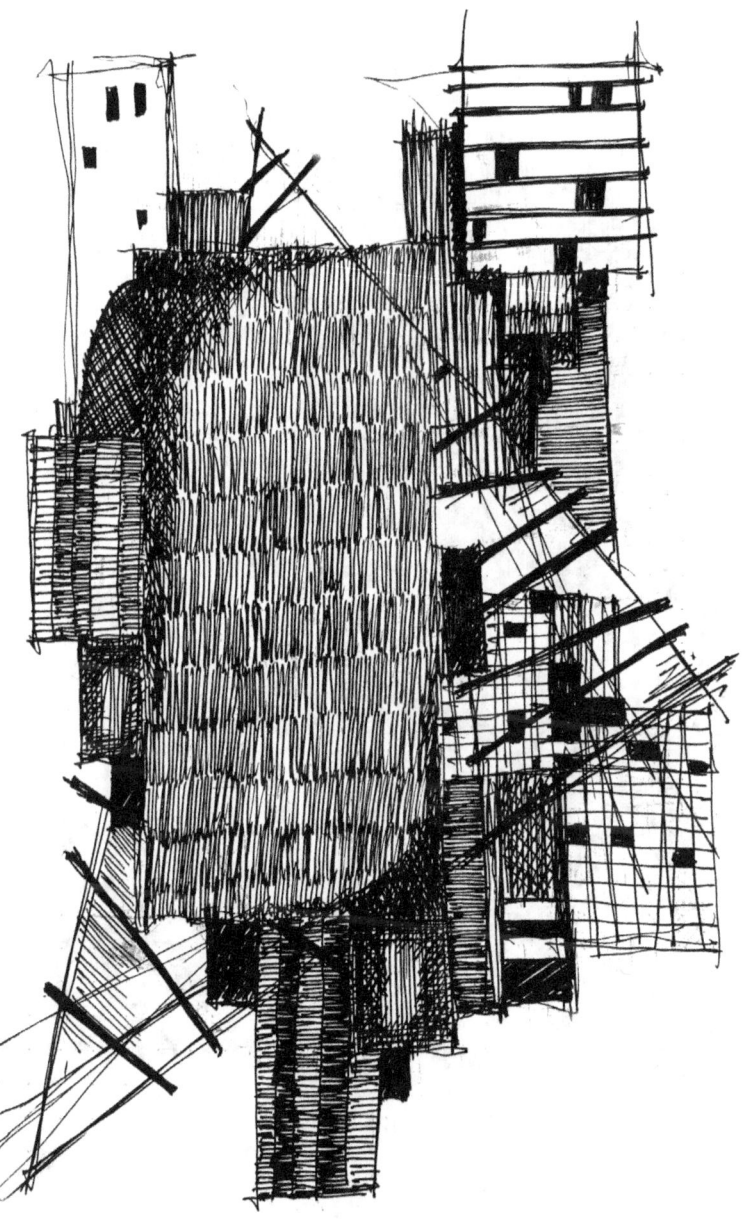

Dana Krystle

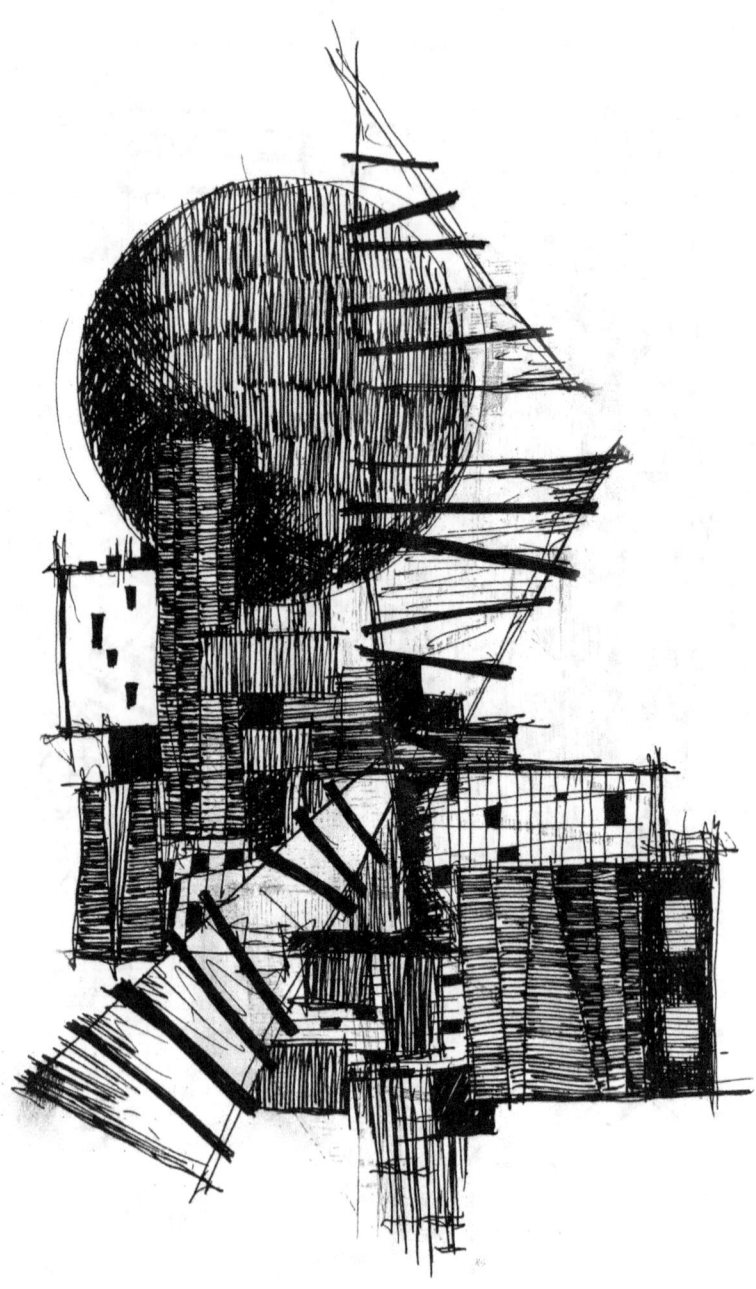

The Monochrome Collection Vol.1

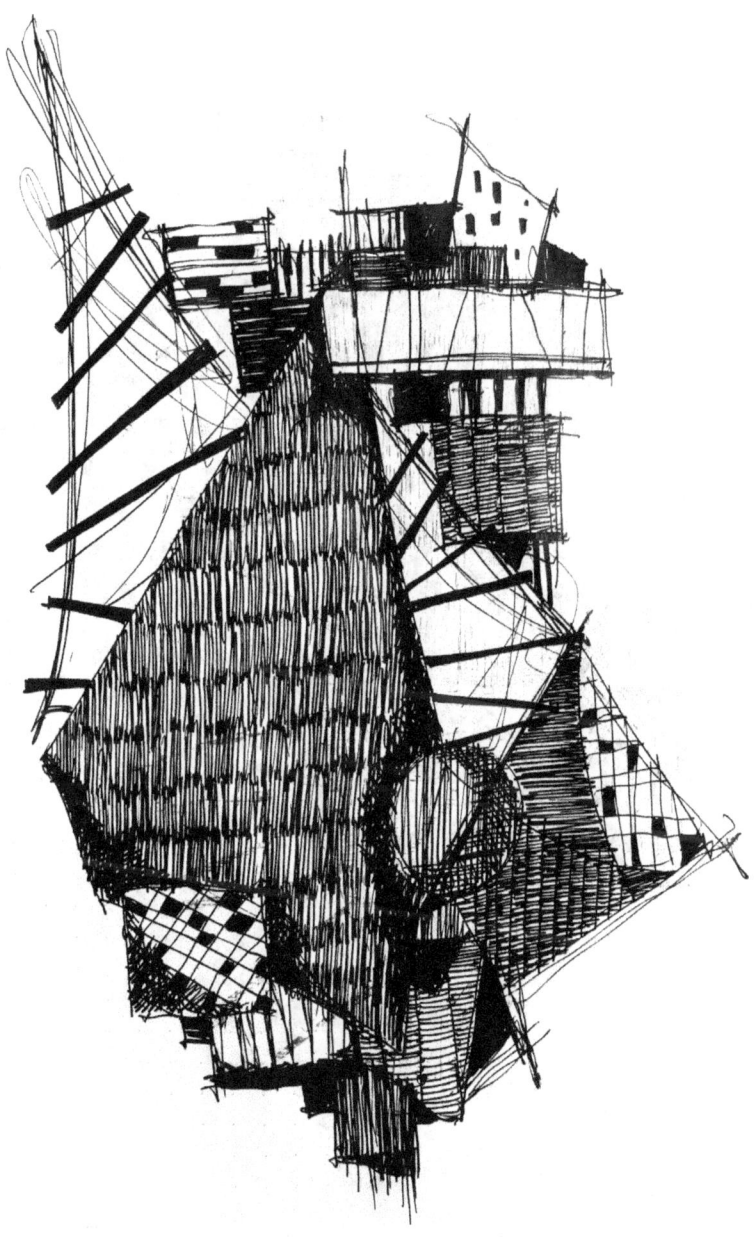

Dana Krystle

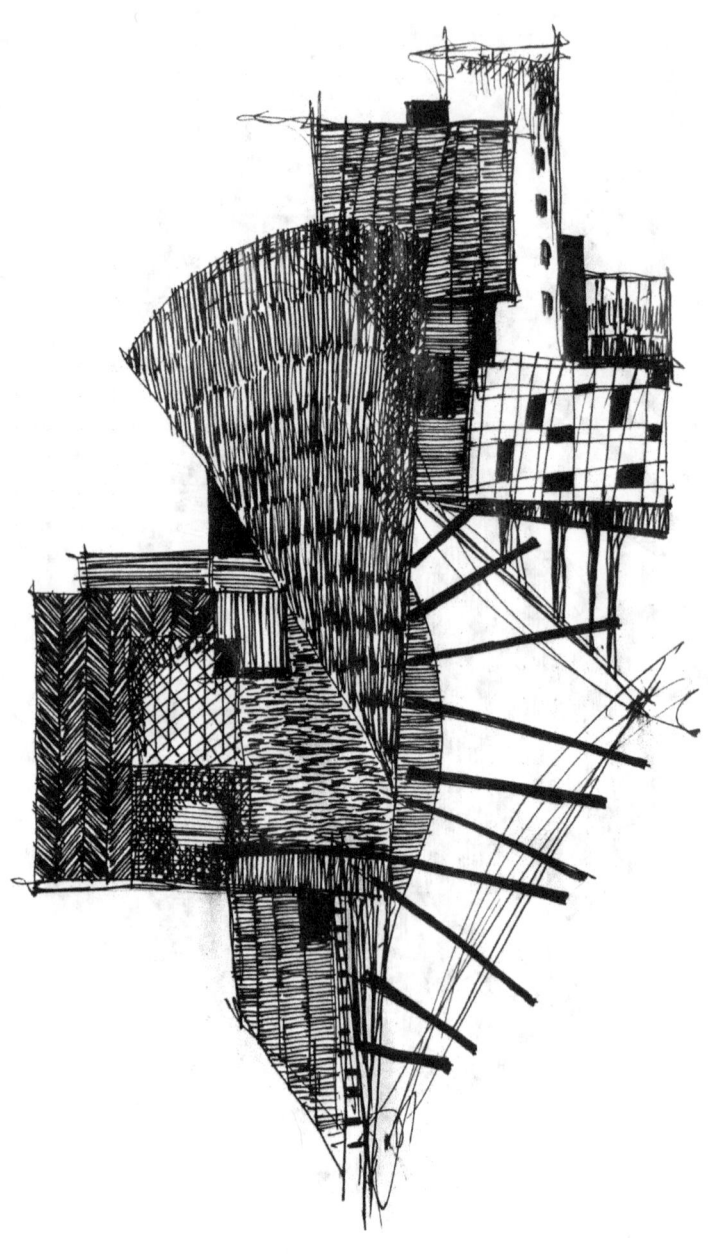

The Monochrome Collection Vol.1

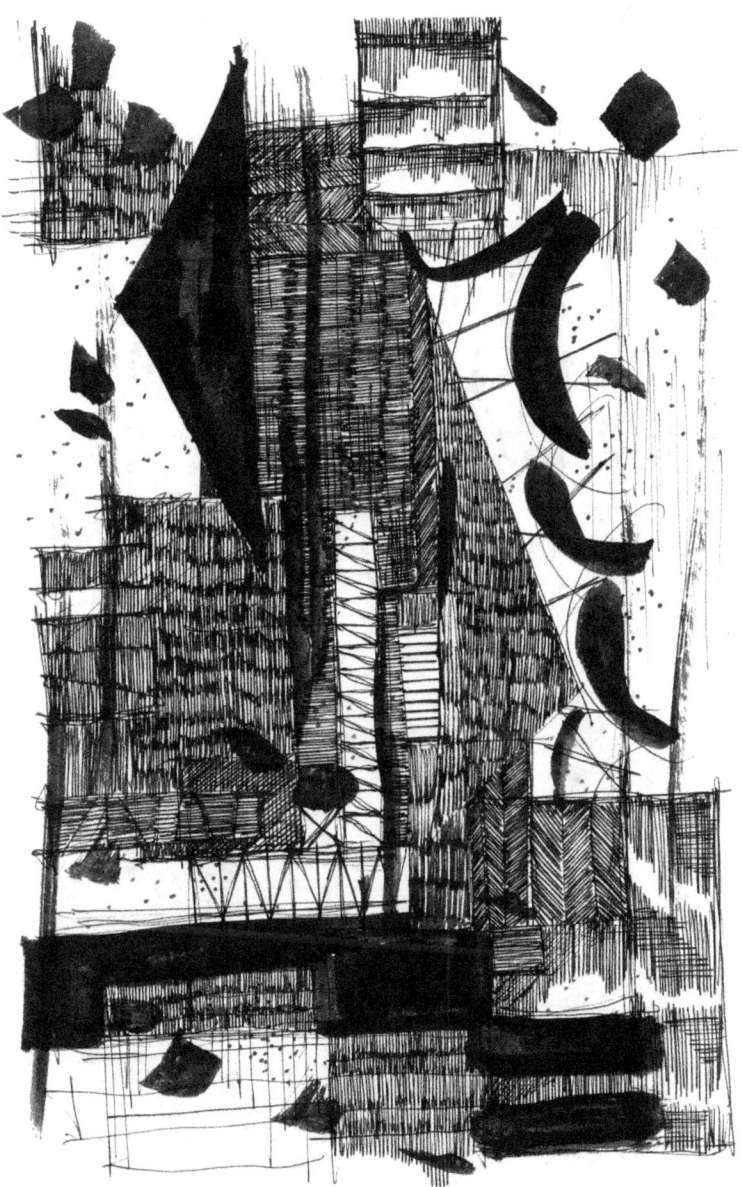

Dana Krystle

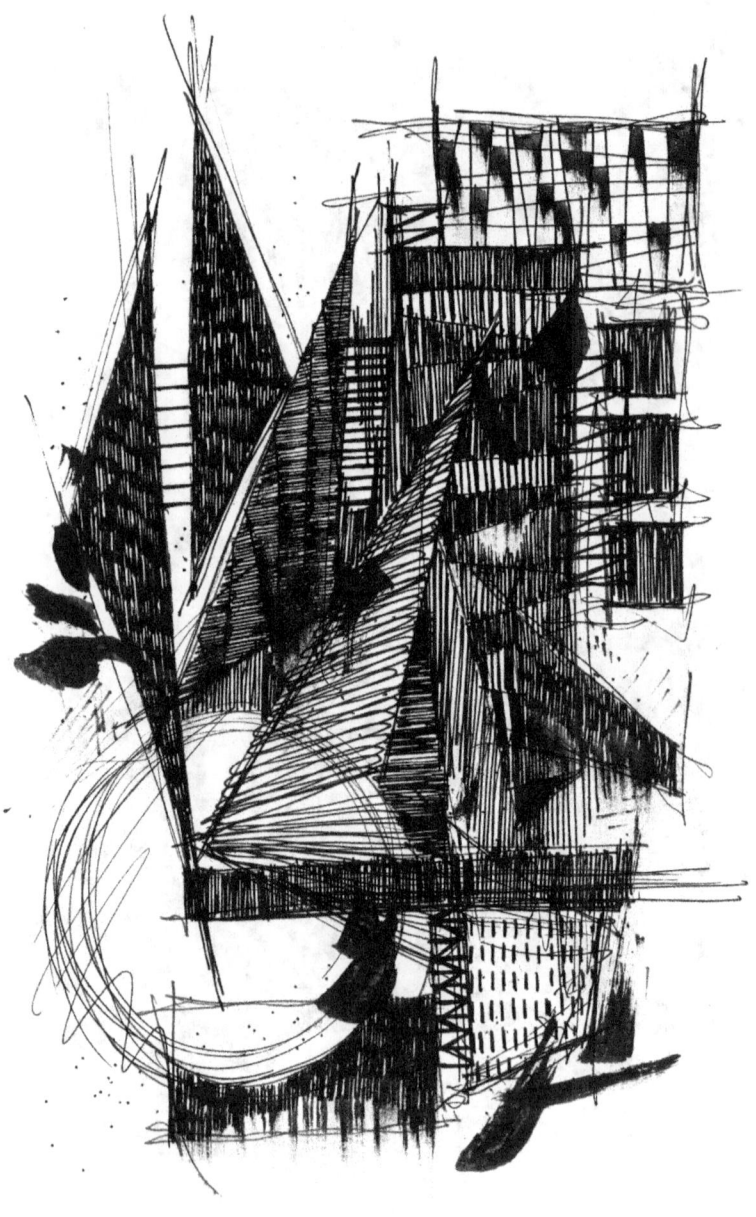

The Monochrome Collection Vol.1

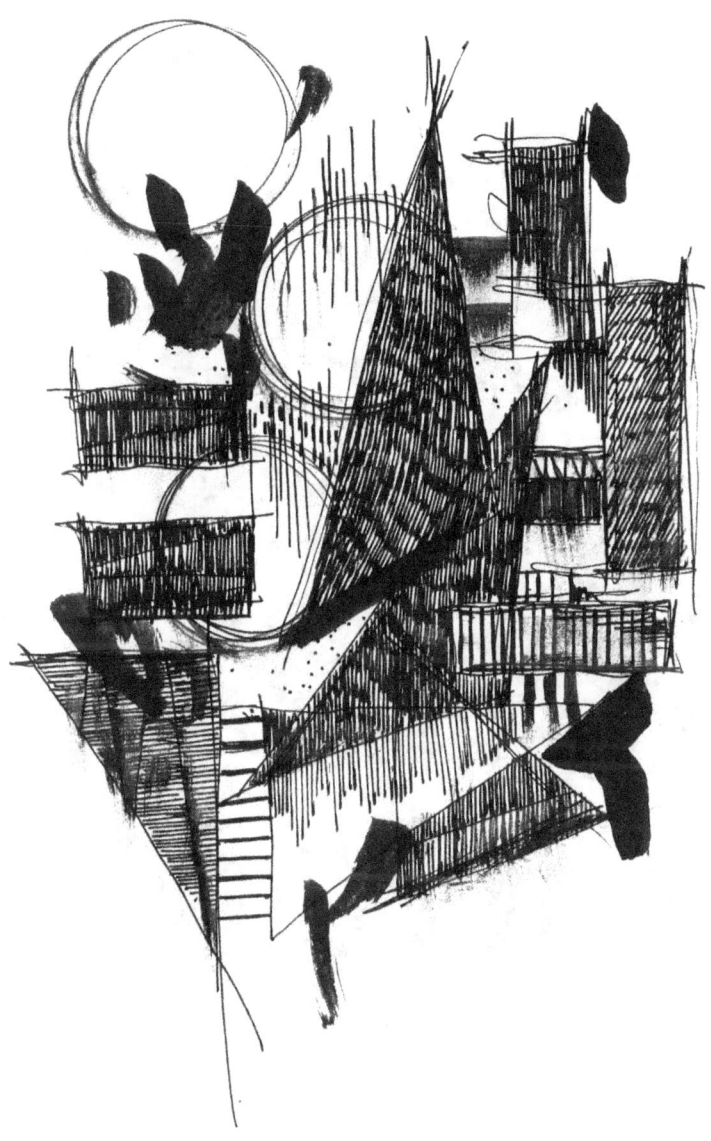

Dana Krystle

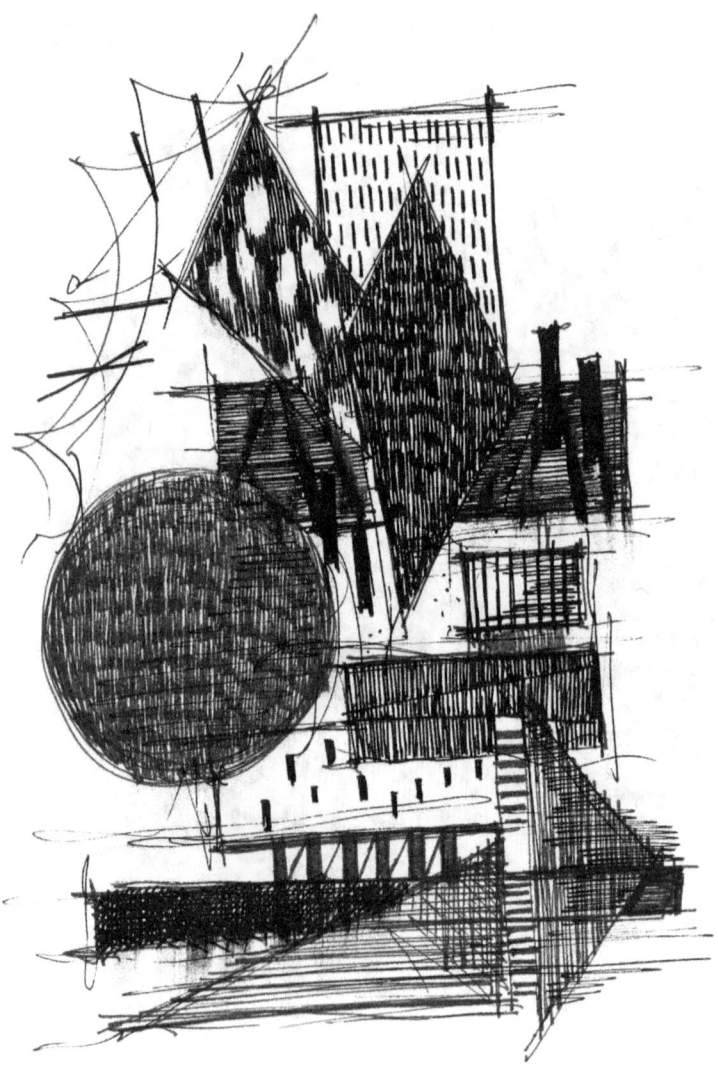

The Monochrome Collection Vol.1

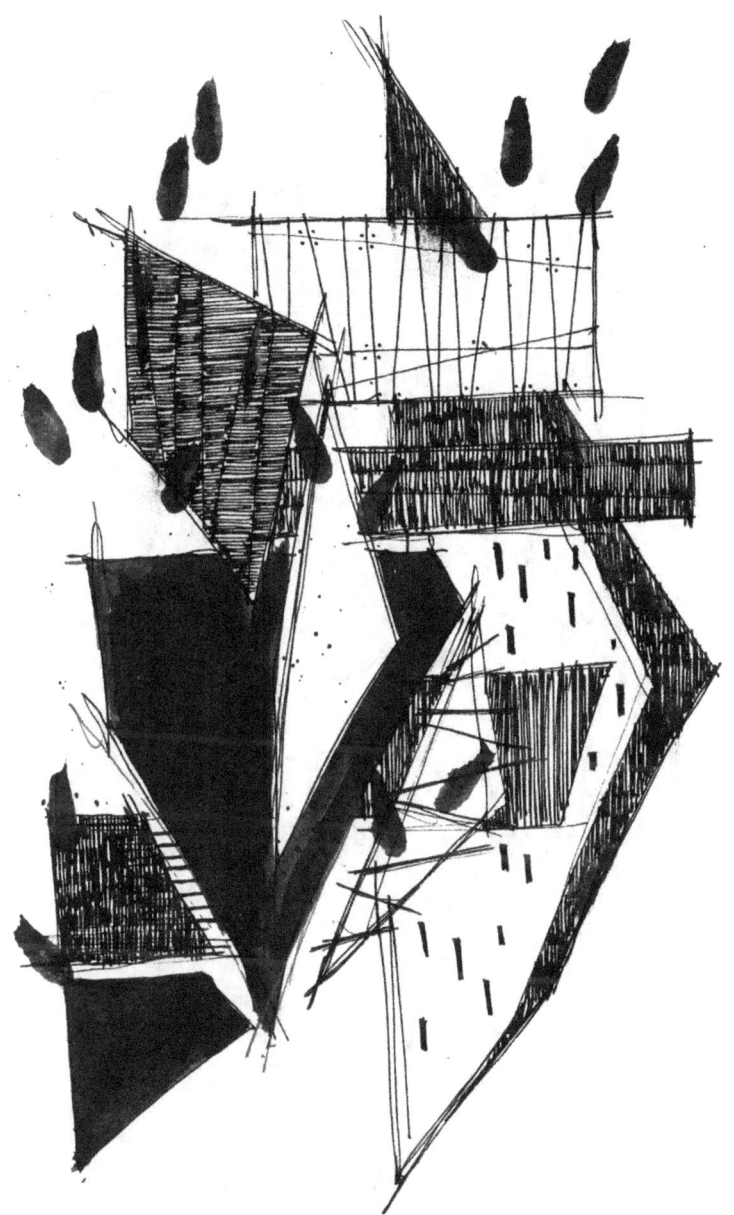

Dana Krystle

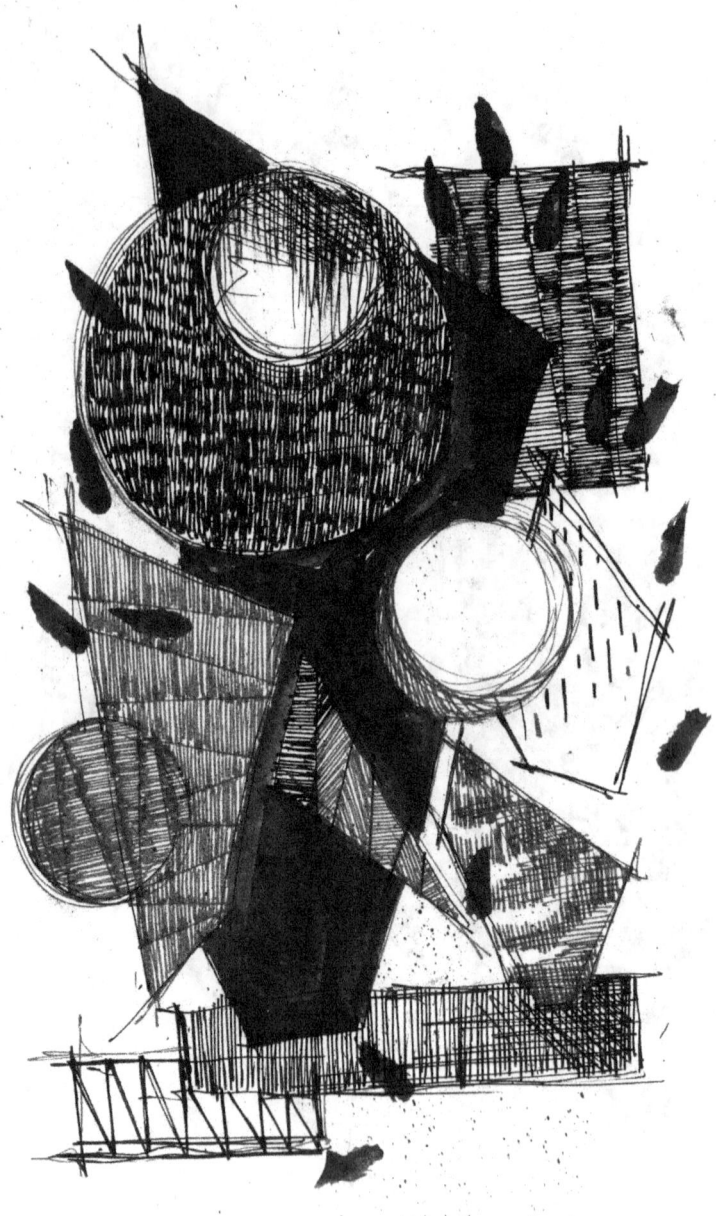

The Monochrome Collection Vol.1

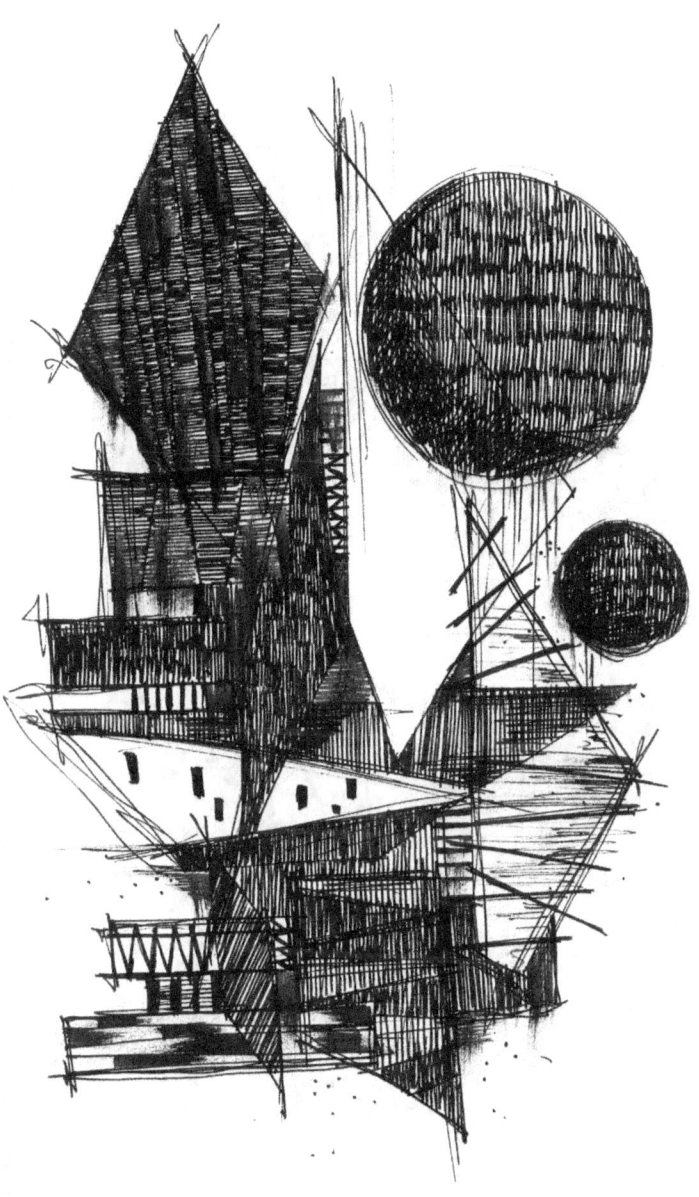

Dana Krystle

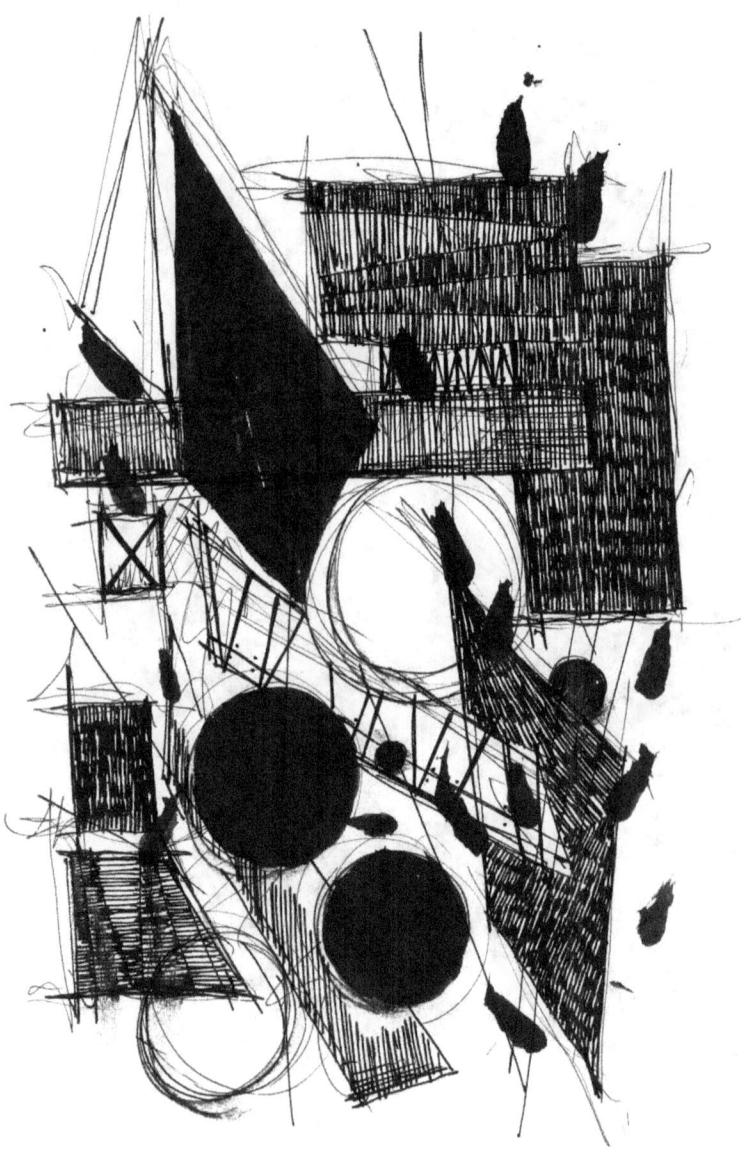

The Monochrome Collection Vol.1

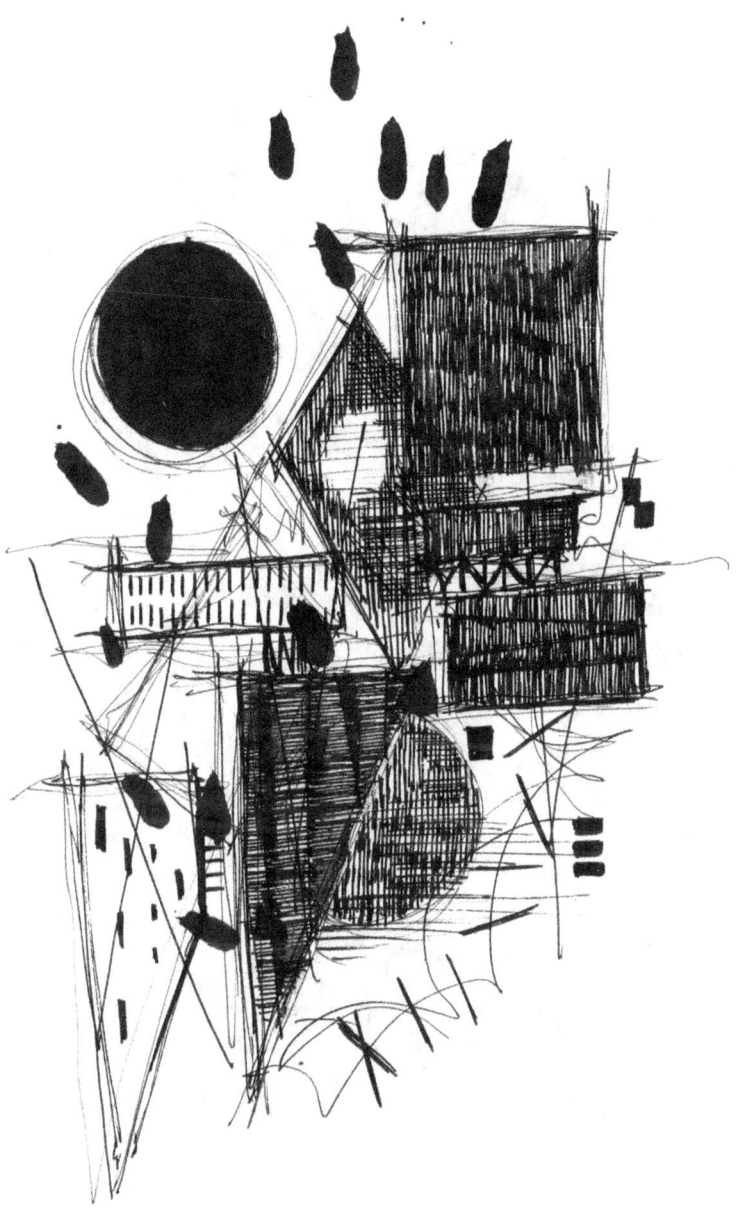

Dana Krystle

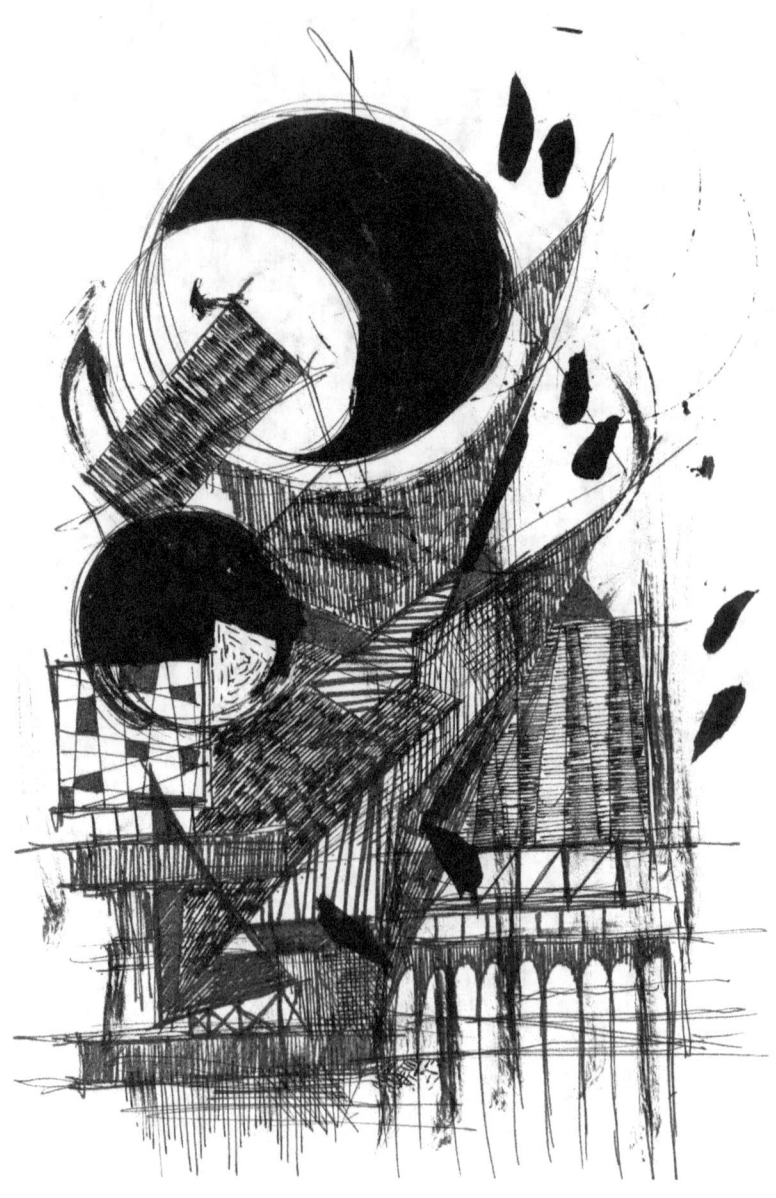

The Monochrome Collection Vol.1

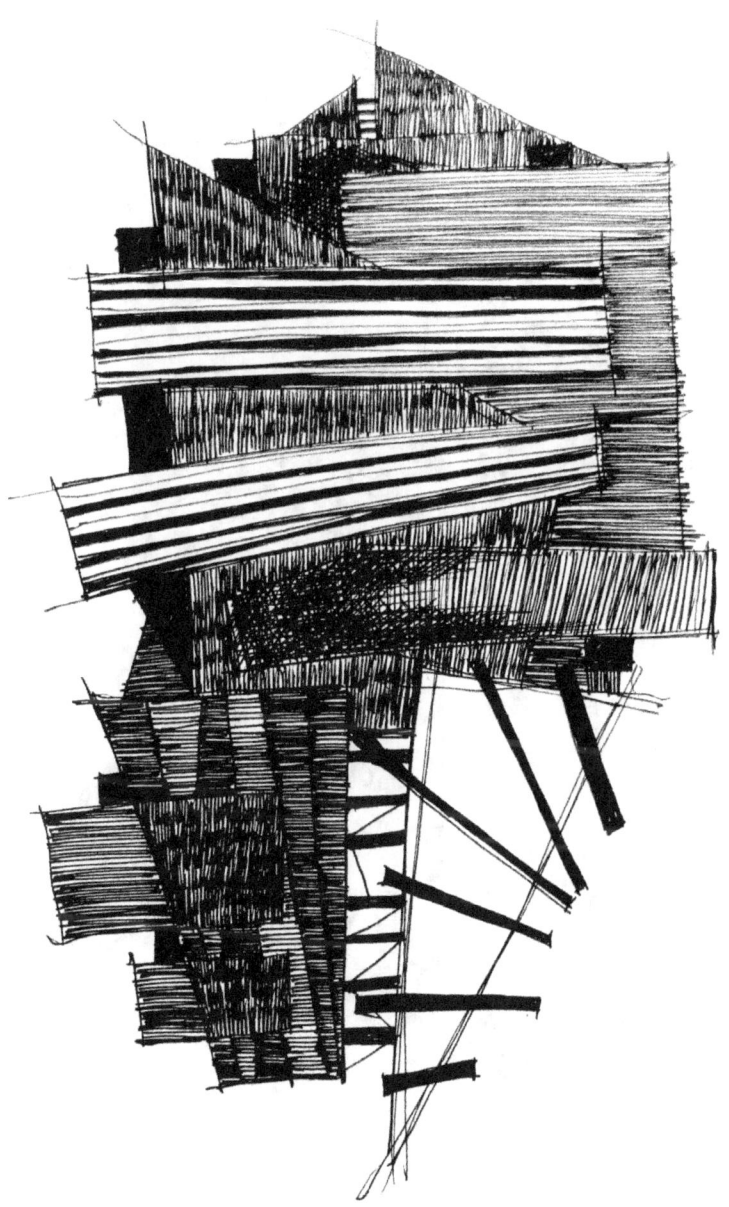

Dana Krystle

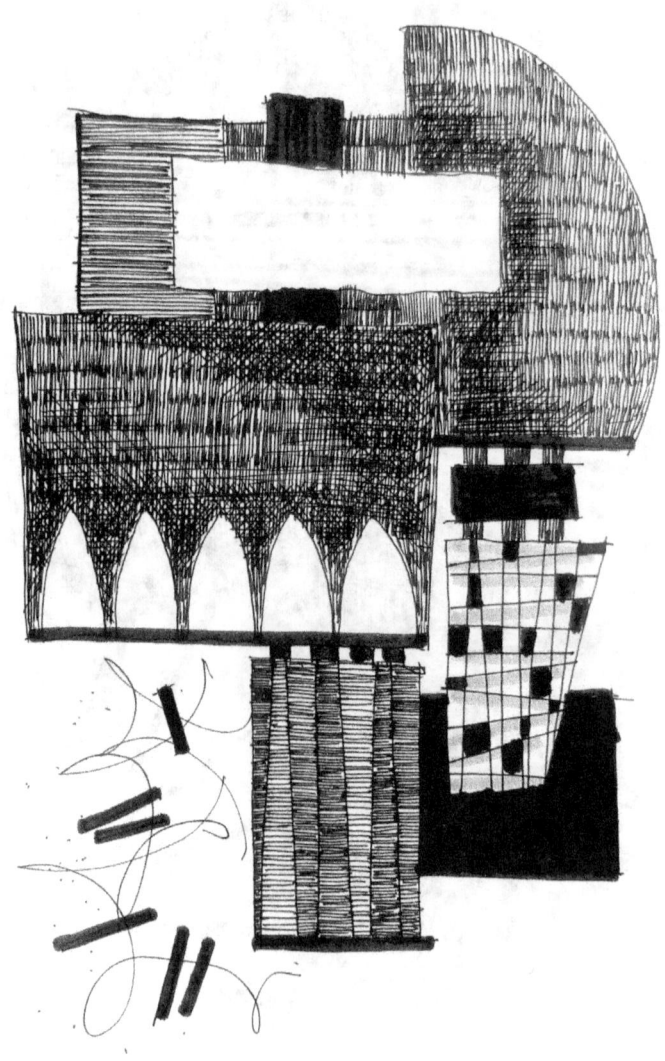

The Monochrome Collection Vol.1

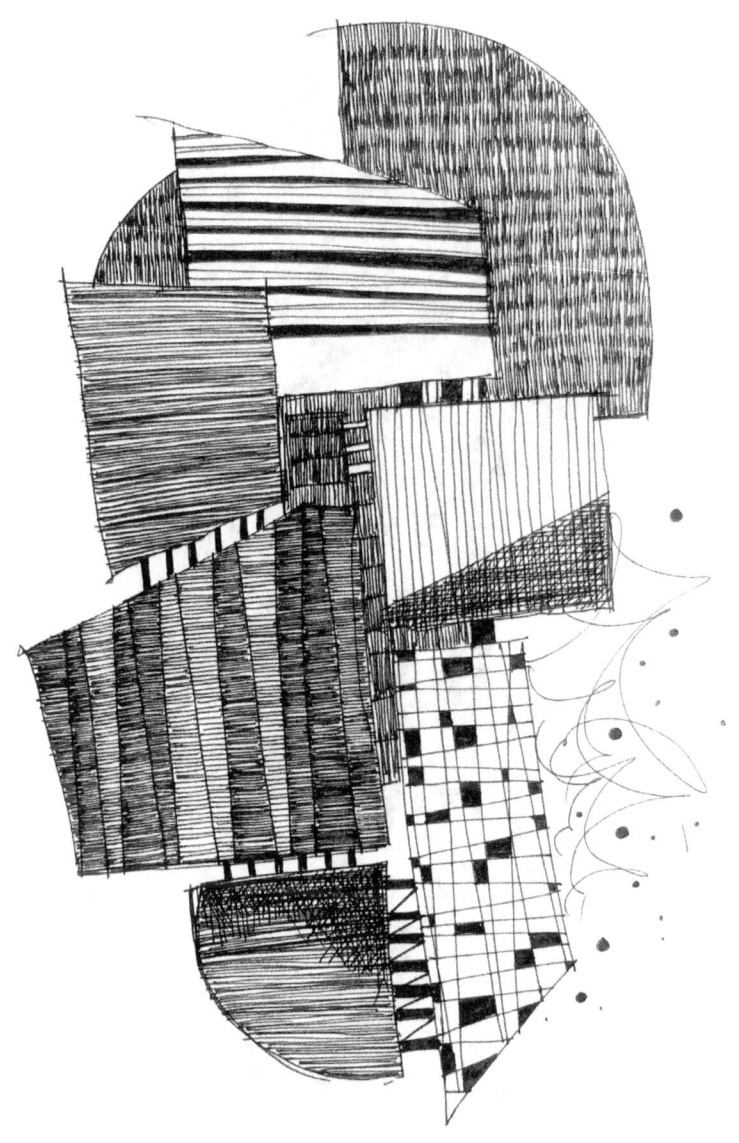

Dana Krystle

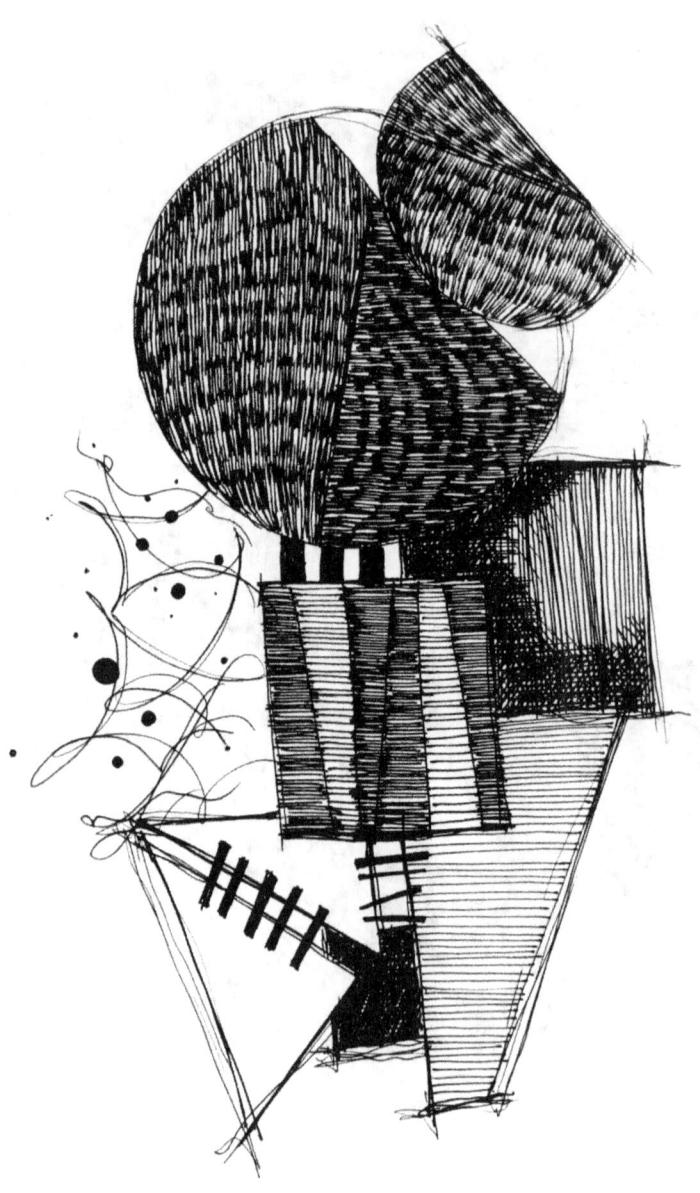

The Monochrome Collection Vol.1

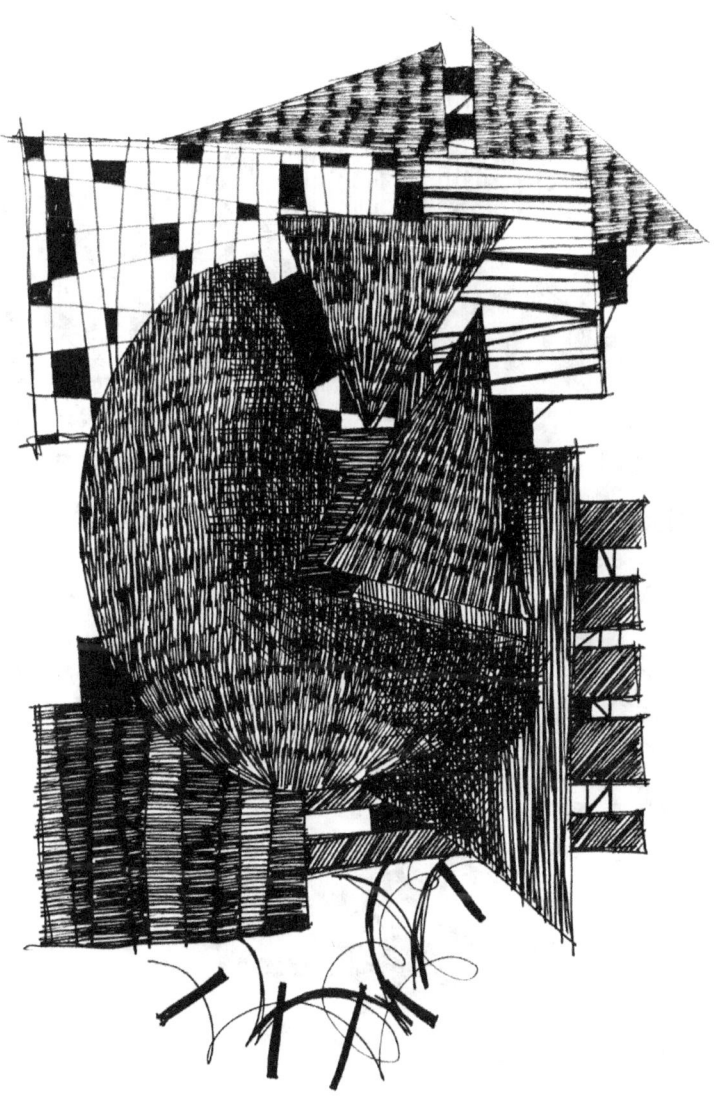

Dana Krystle

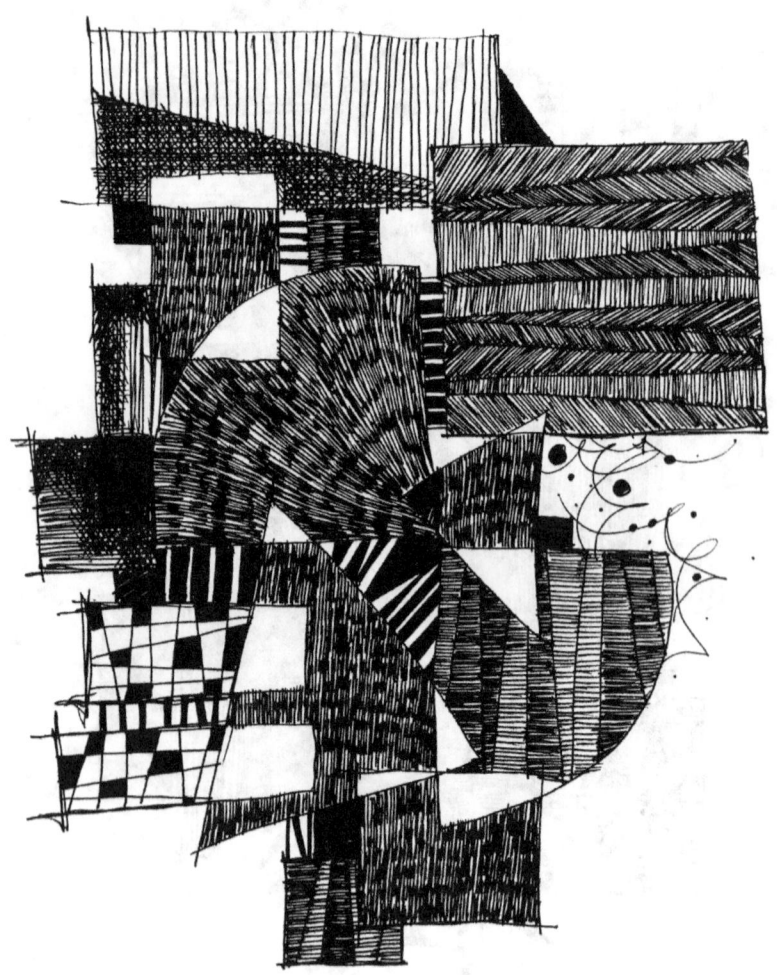

The Monochrome Collection Vol.1

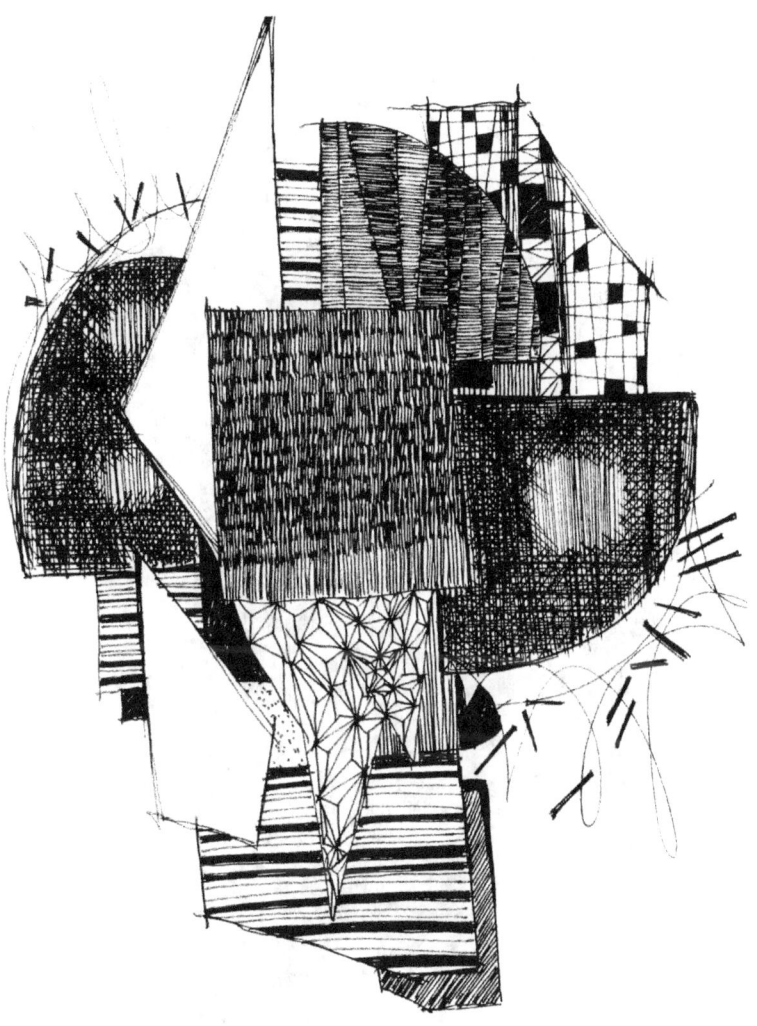

Dana Krystle

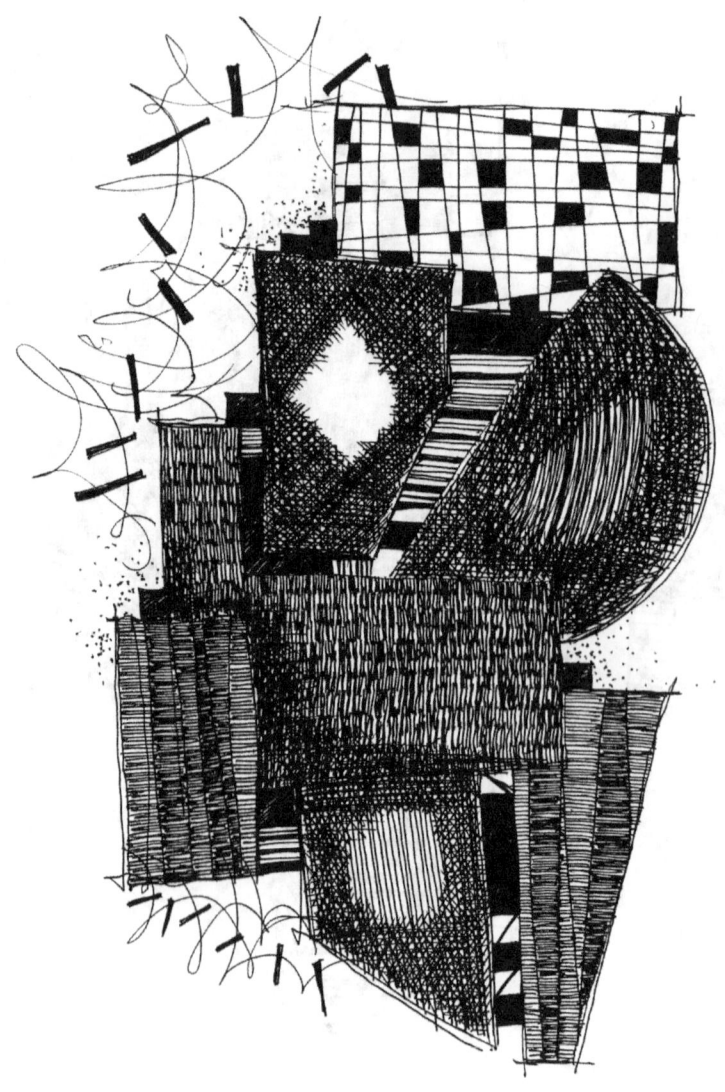

The Monochrome Collection Vol.1

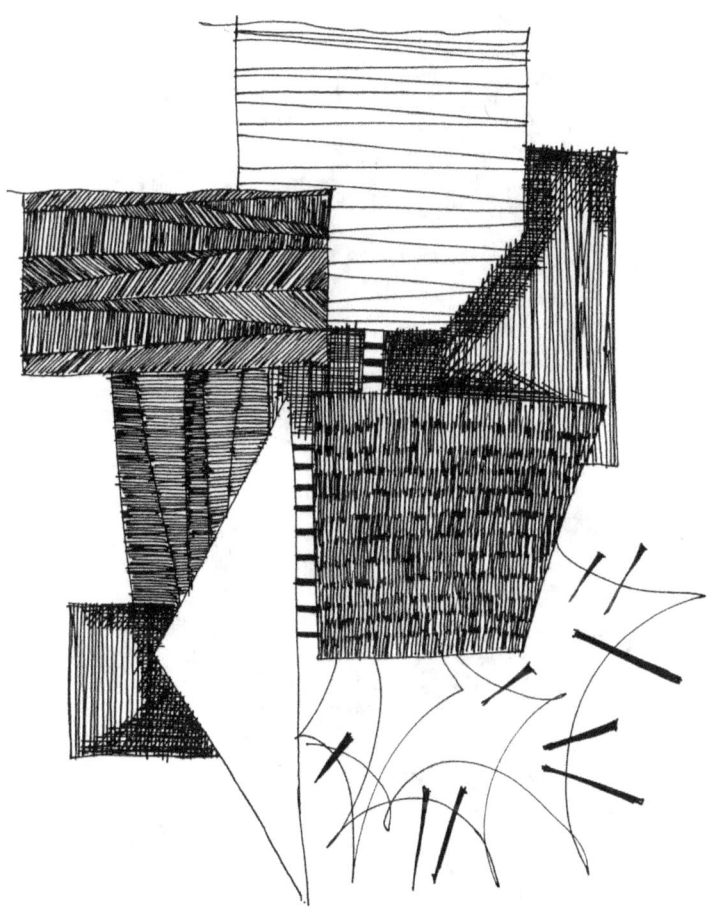

Dana Krystle

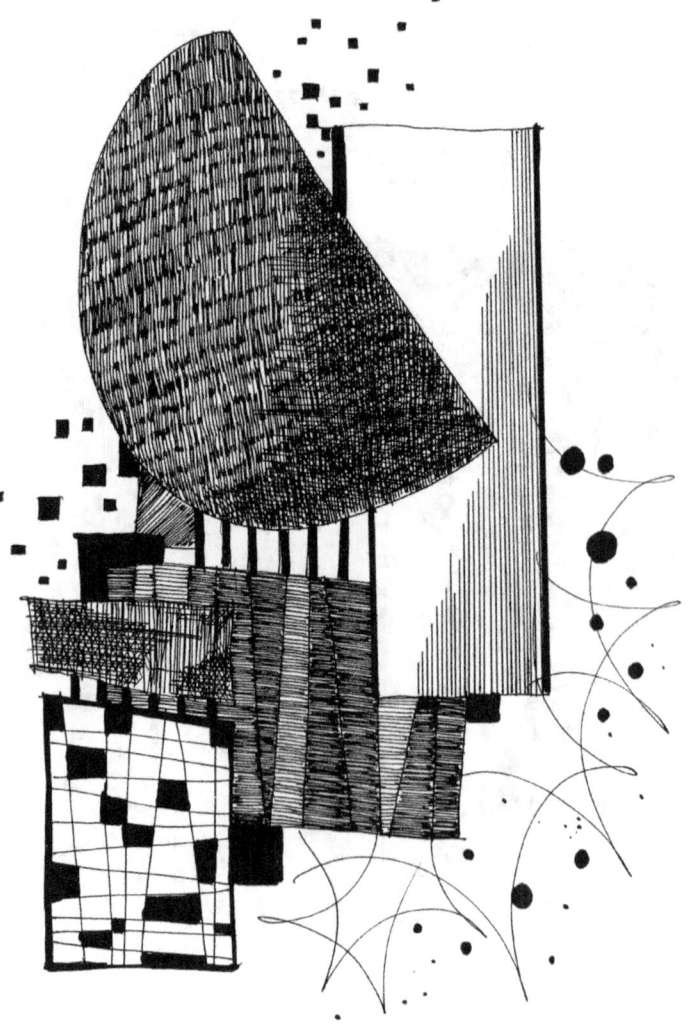

The Monochrome Collection Vol.1

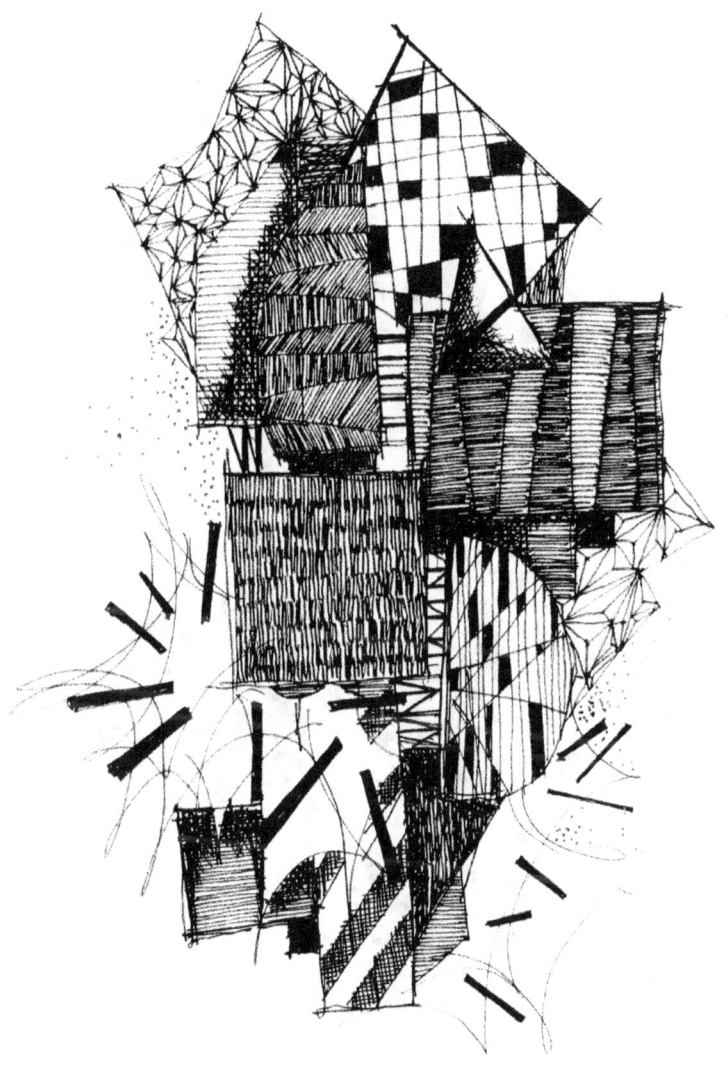

Dana Krystle

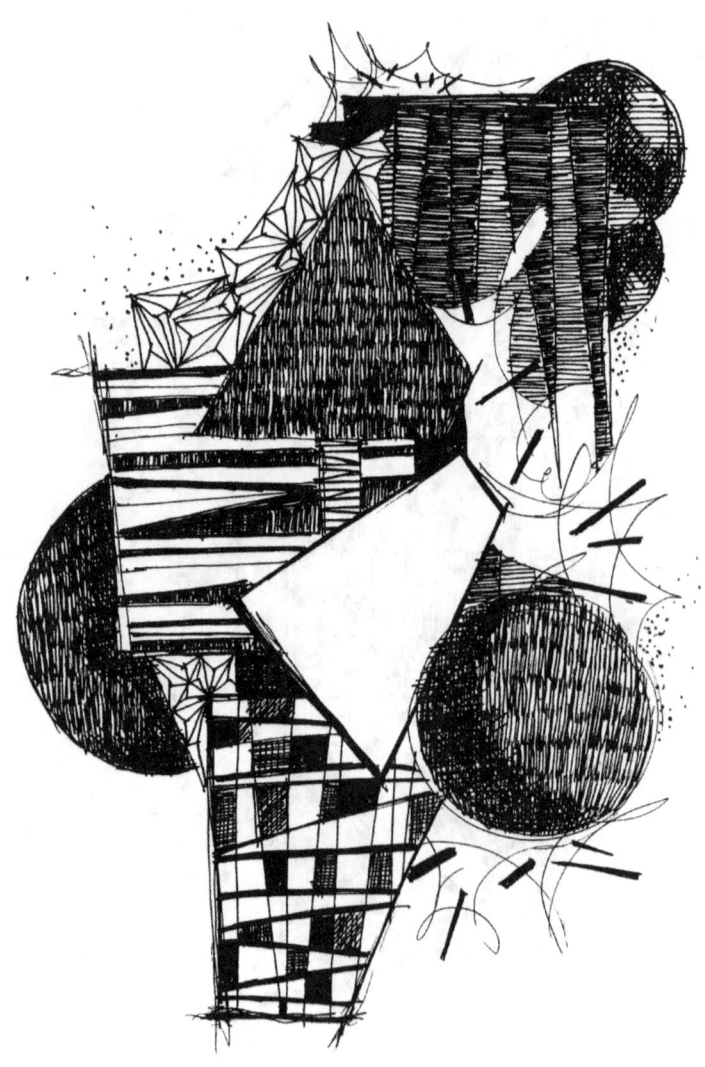

The Monochrome Collection Vol.1

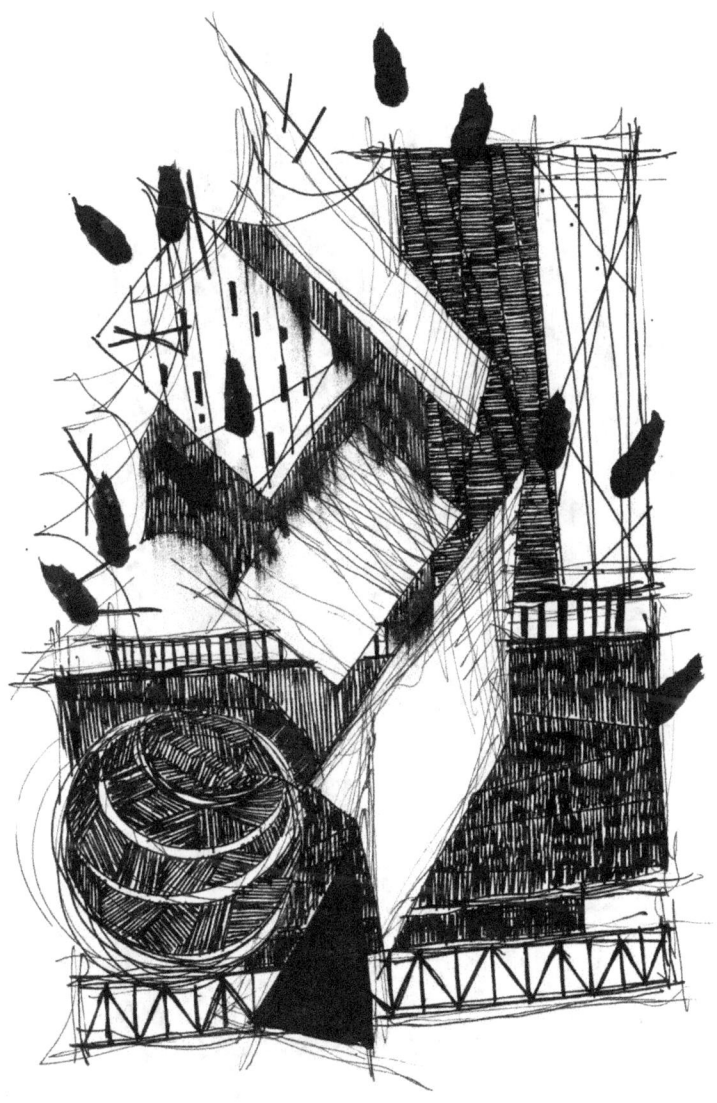

Dana Krystle

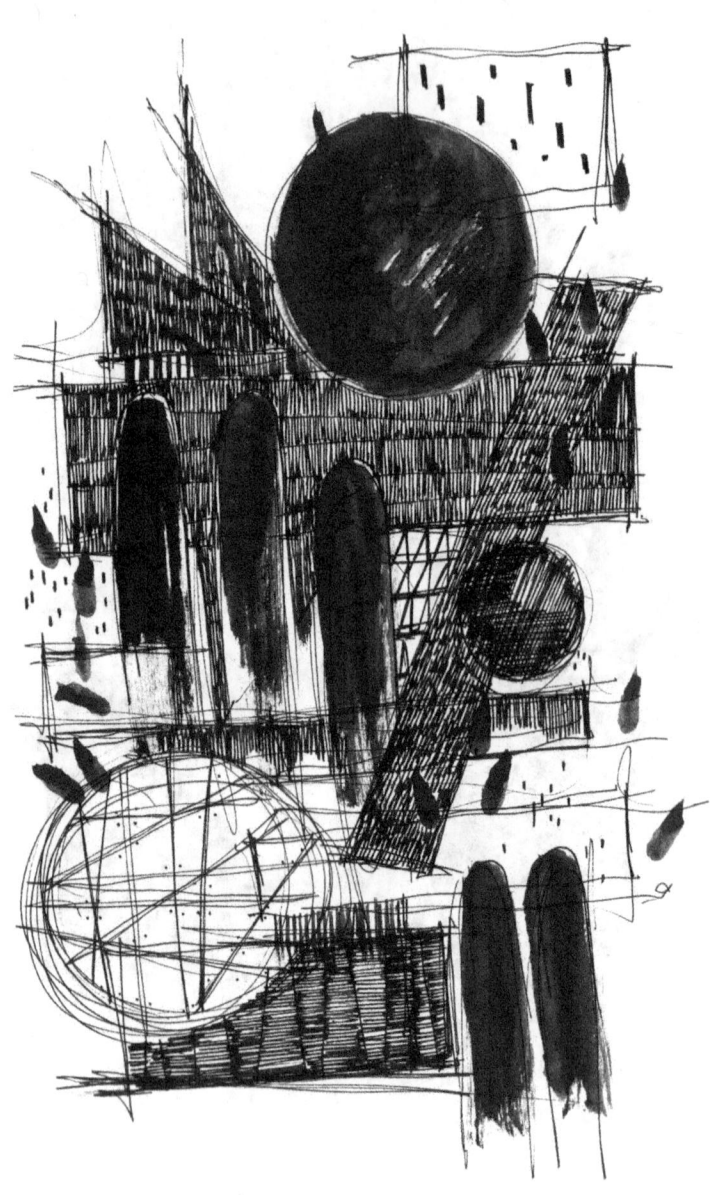

The Monochrome Collection Vol.1

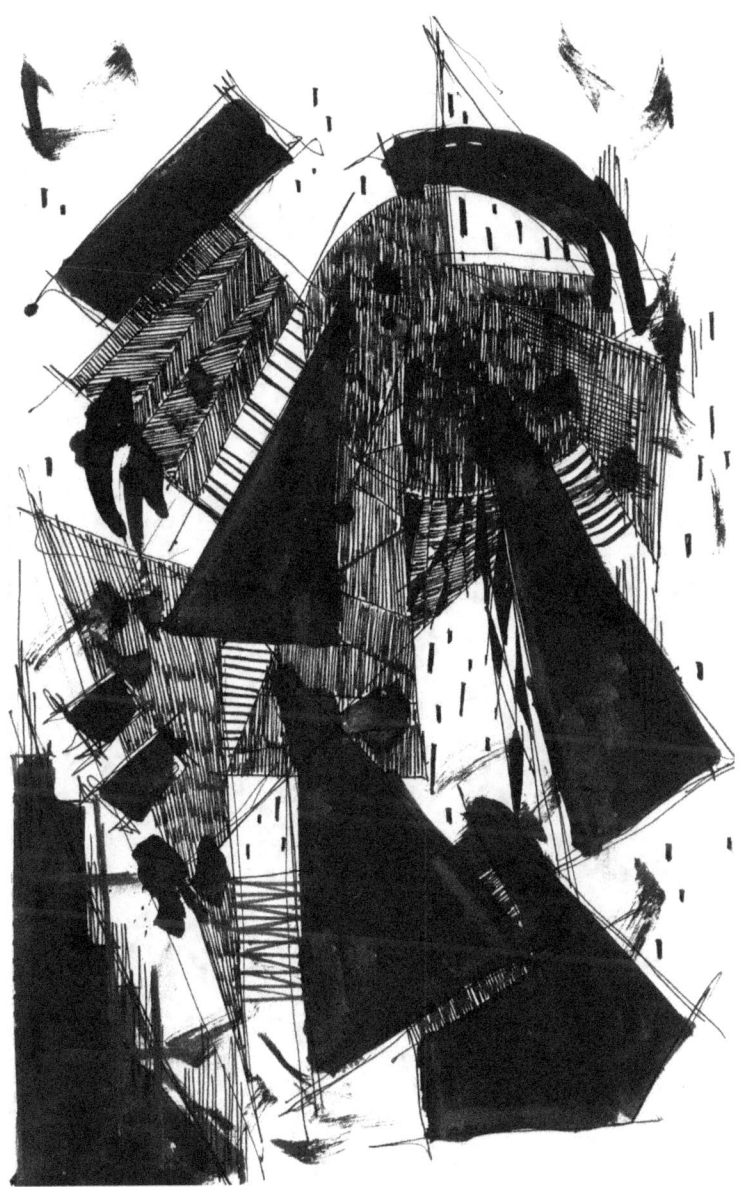

Dana Krystle

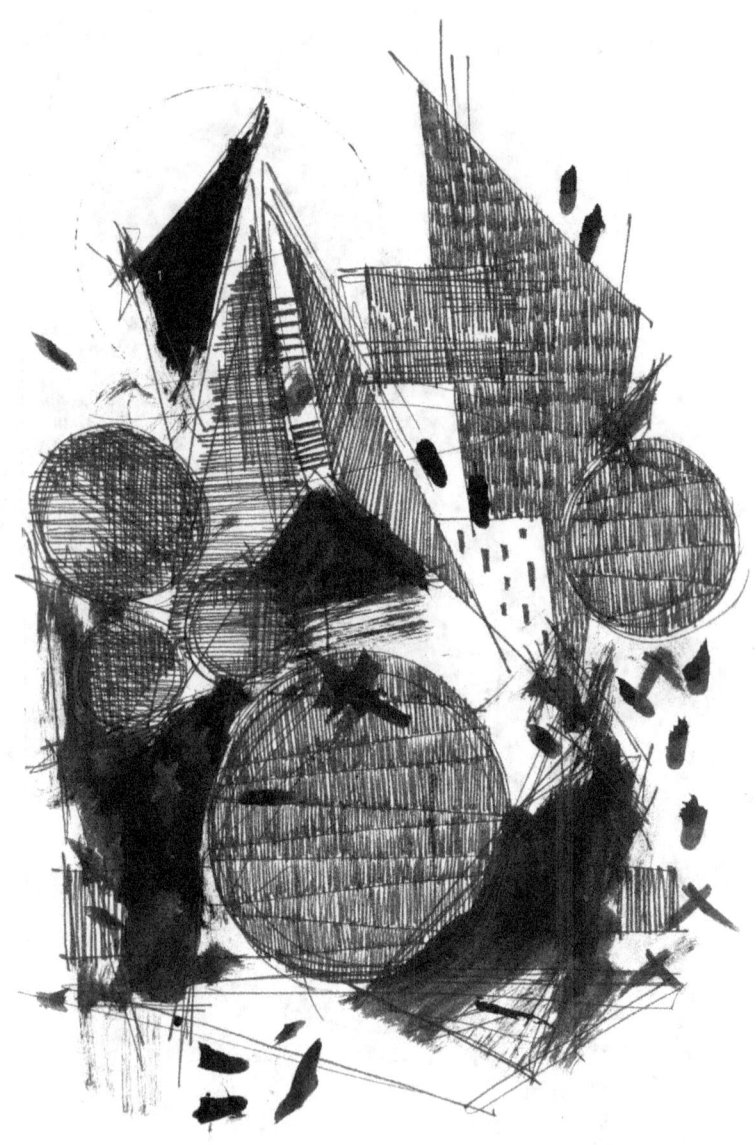

The Monochrome Collection Vol.1

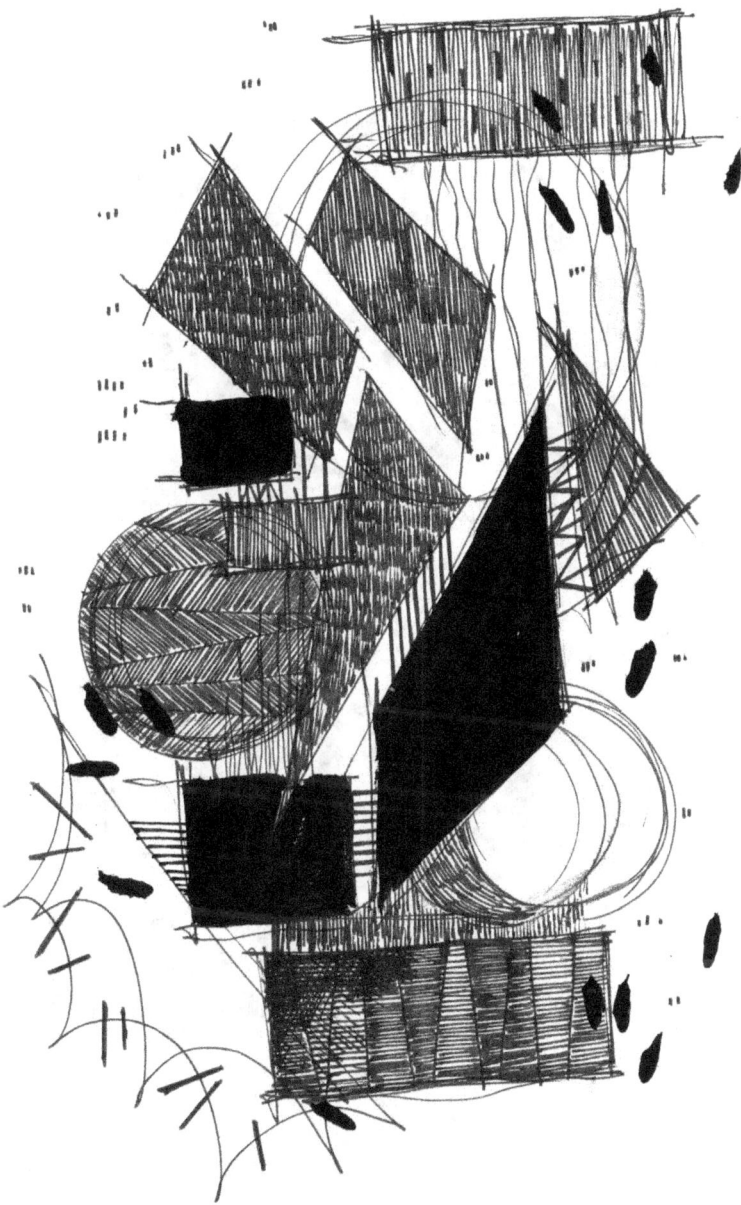

Dana Krystle

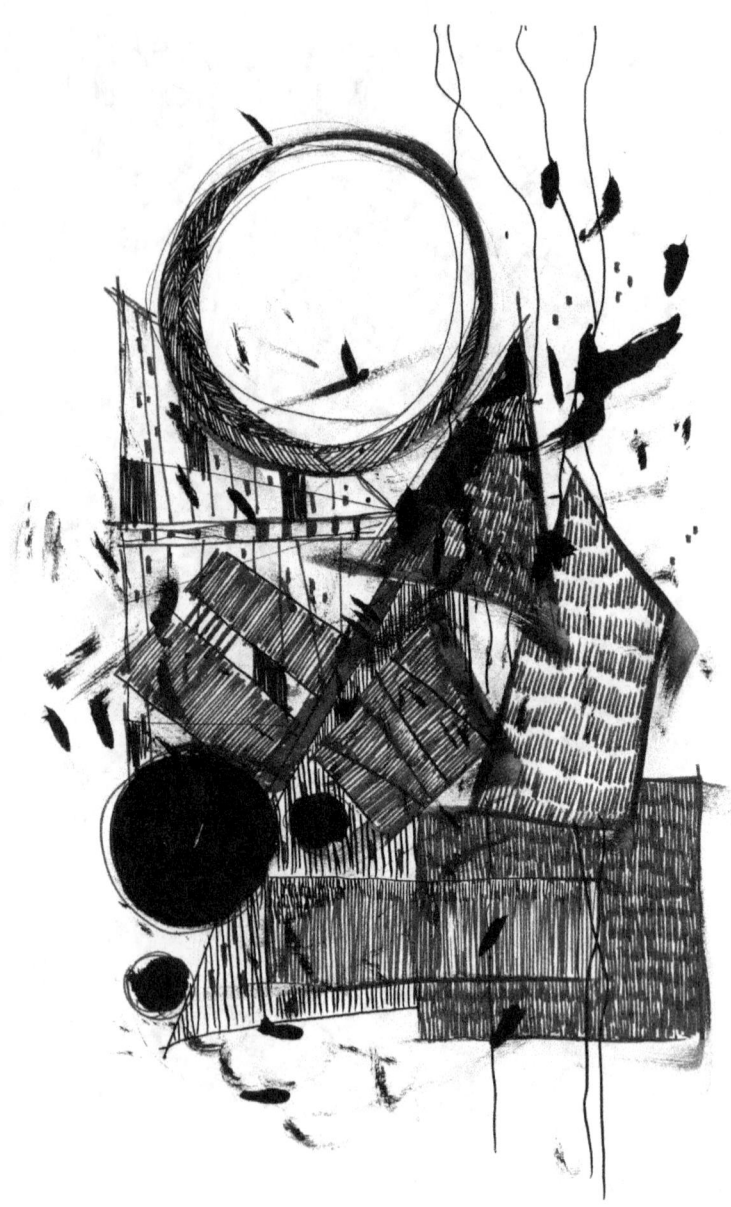

The Monochrome Collection Vol.1

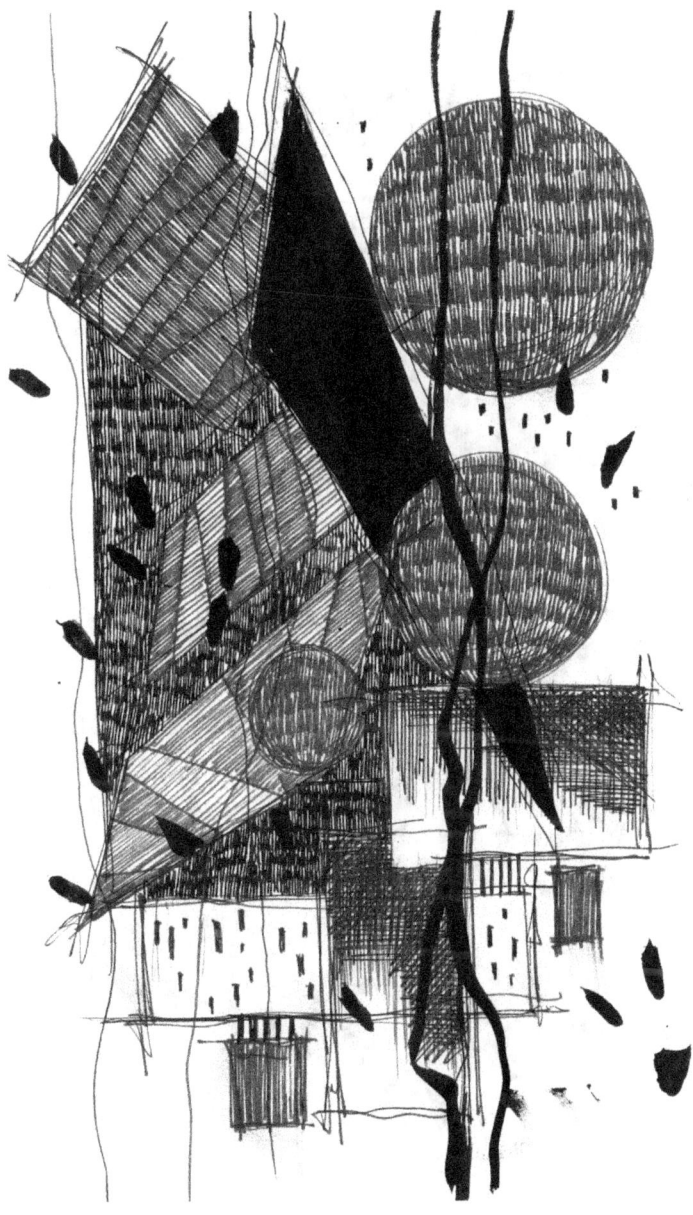

Dana Krystle

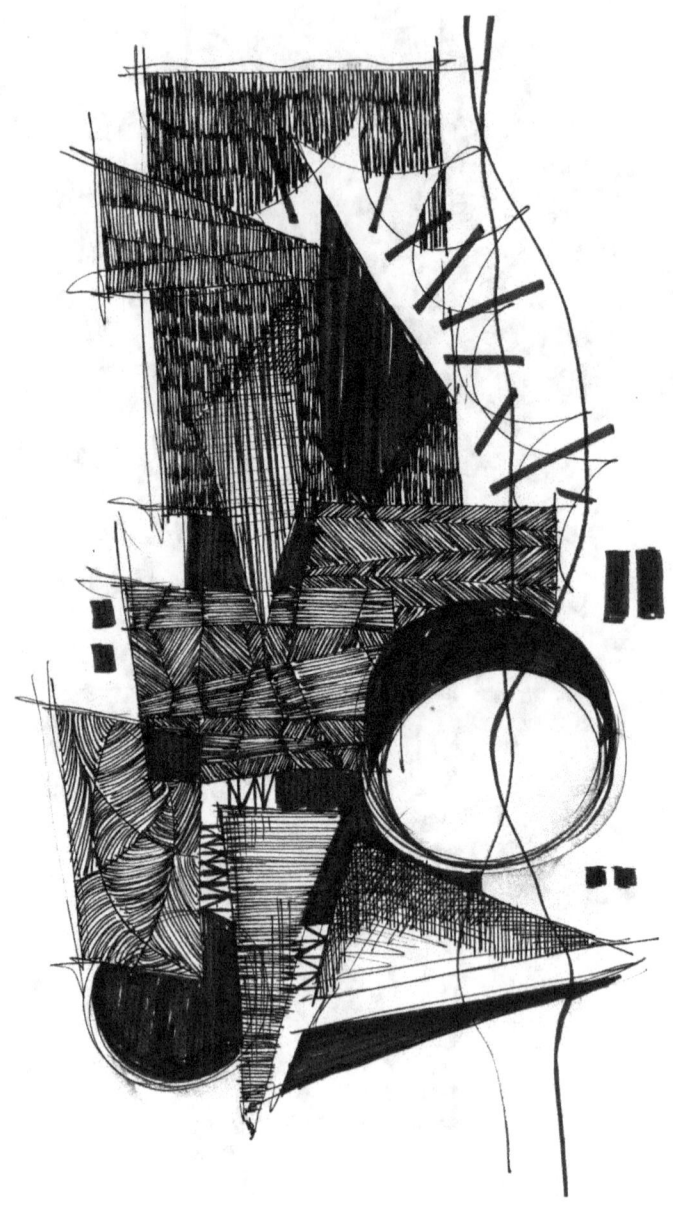

The Monochrome Collection Vol.1

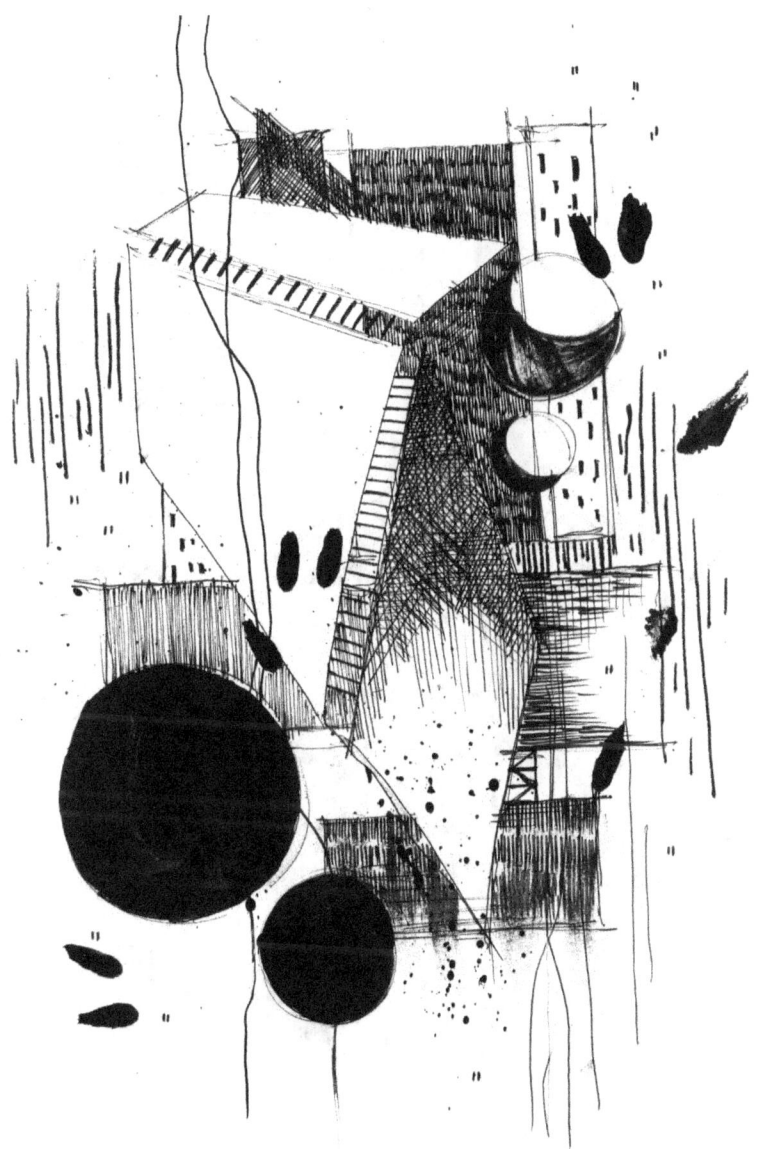

Dana Krystle

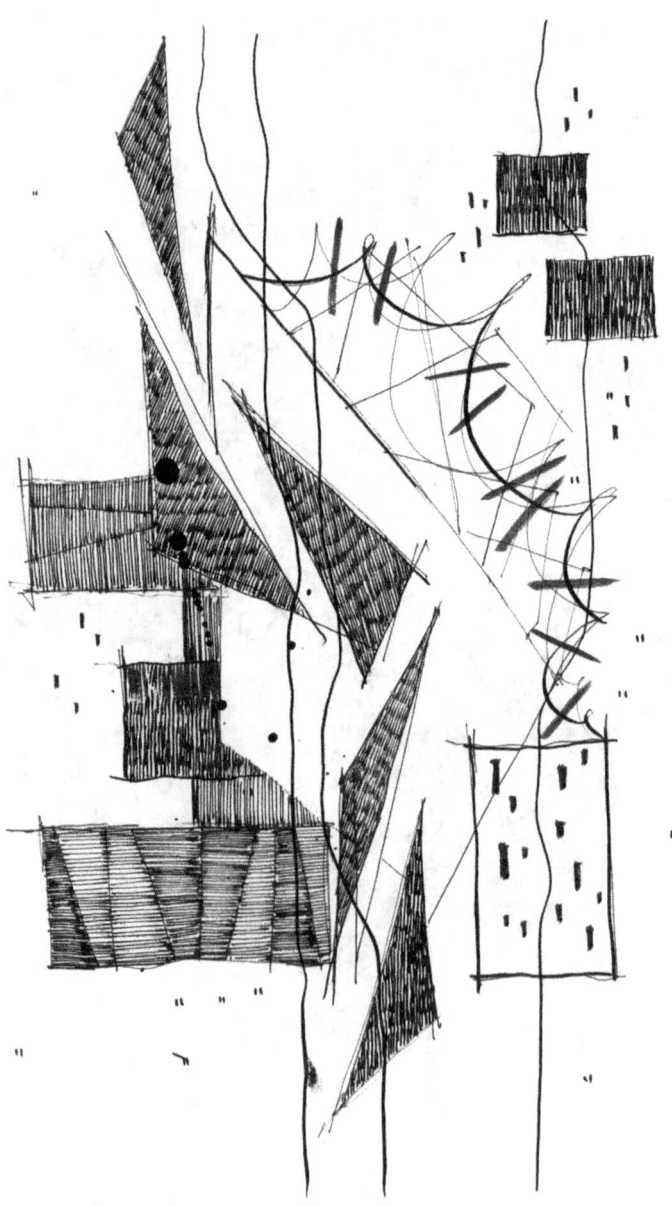

The Monochrome Collection Vol.1

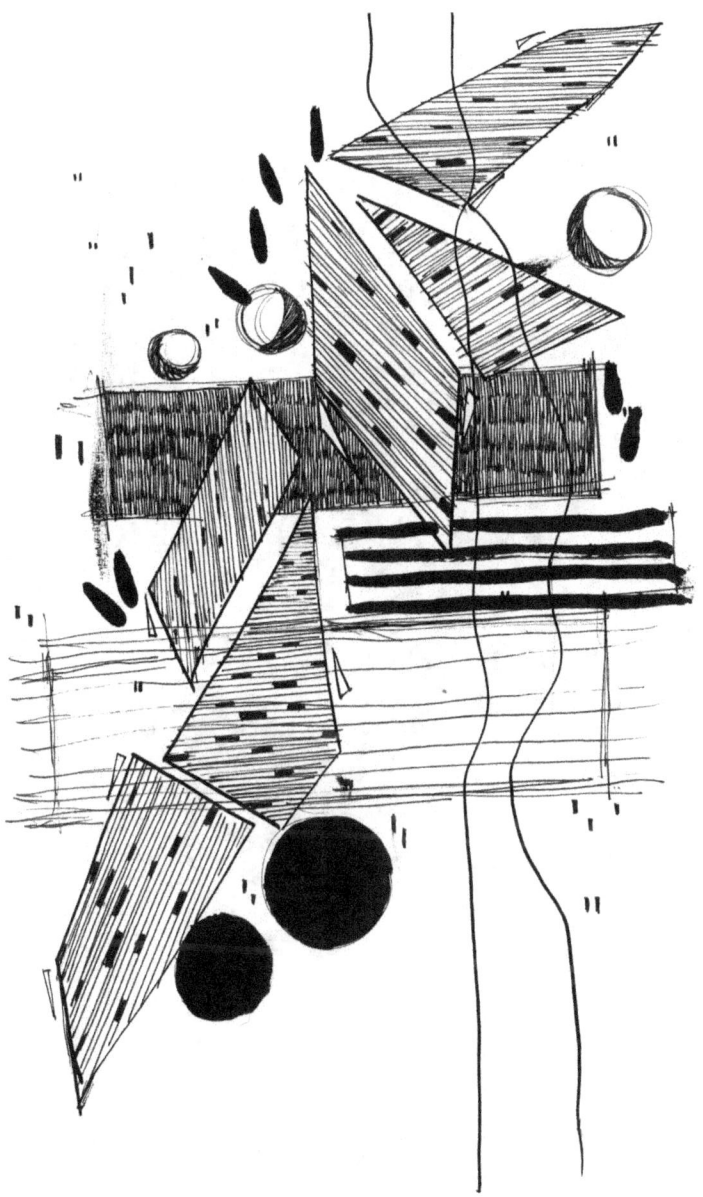

Dana Krystle

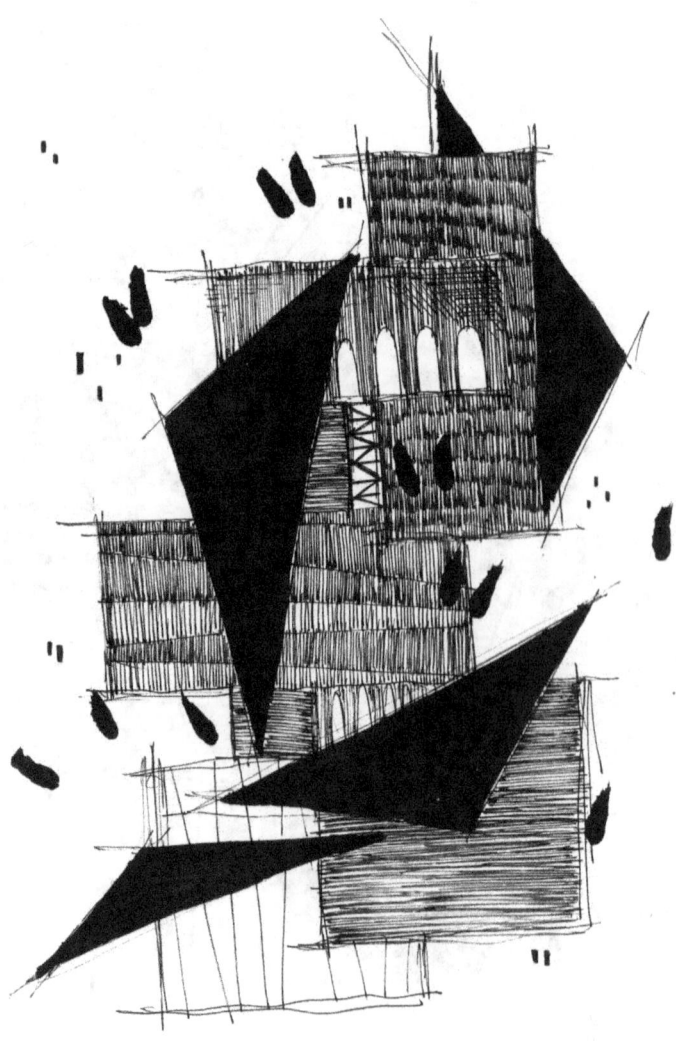

The Monochrome Collection Vol.1

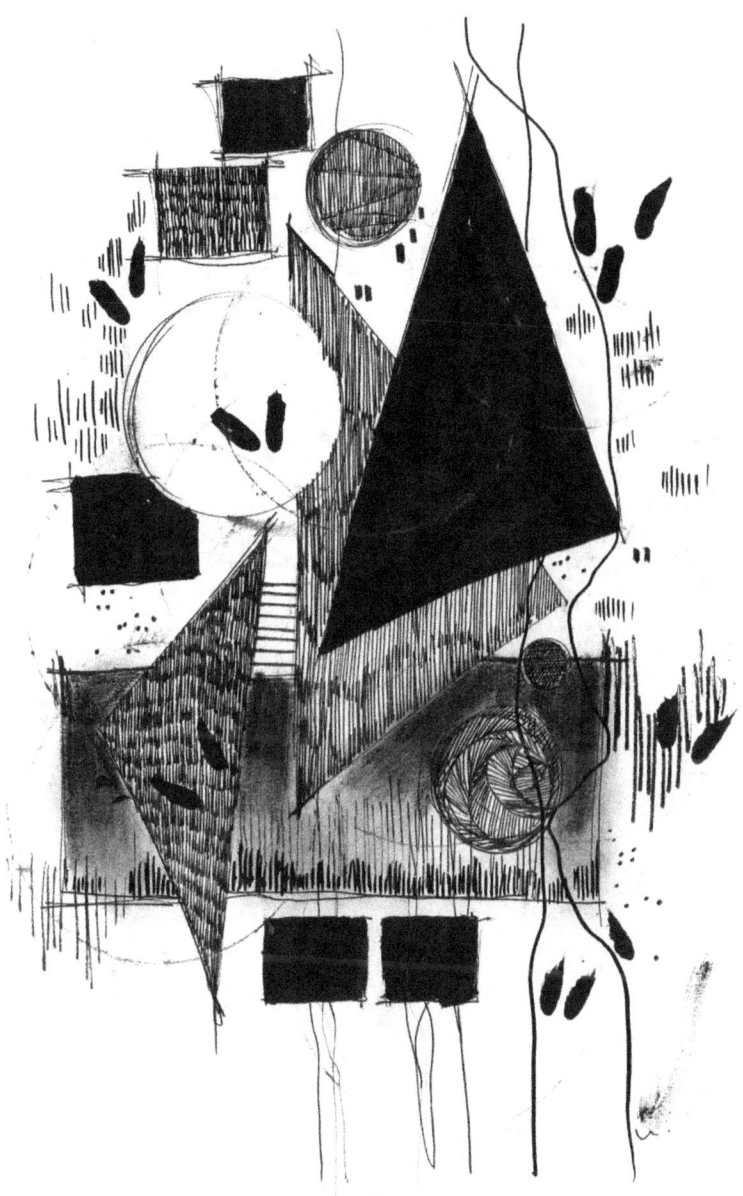

Dana Krystle

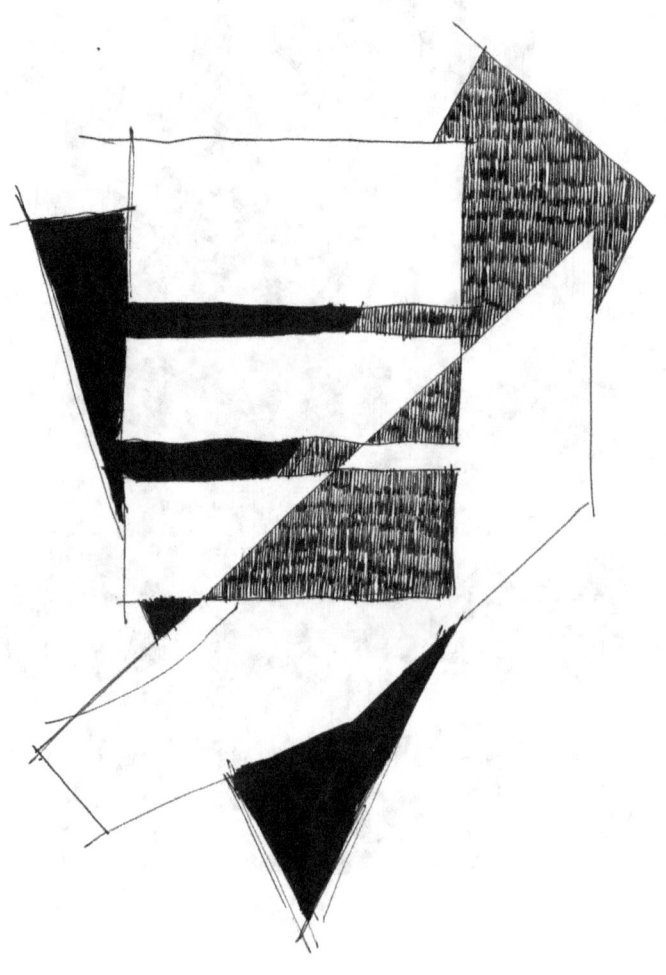

The Monochrome Collection Vol.1

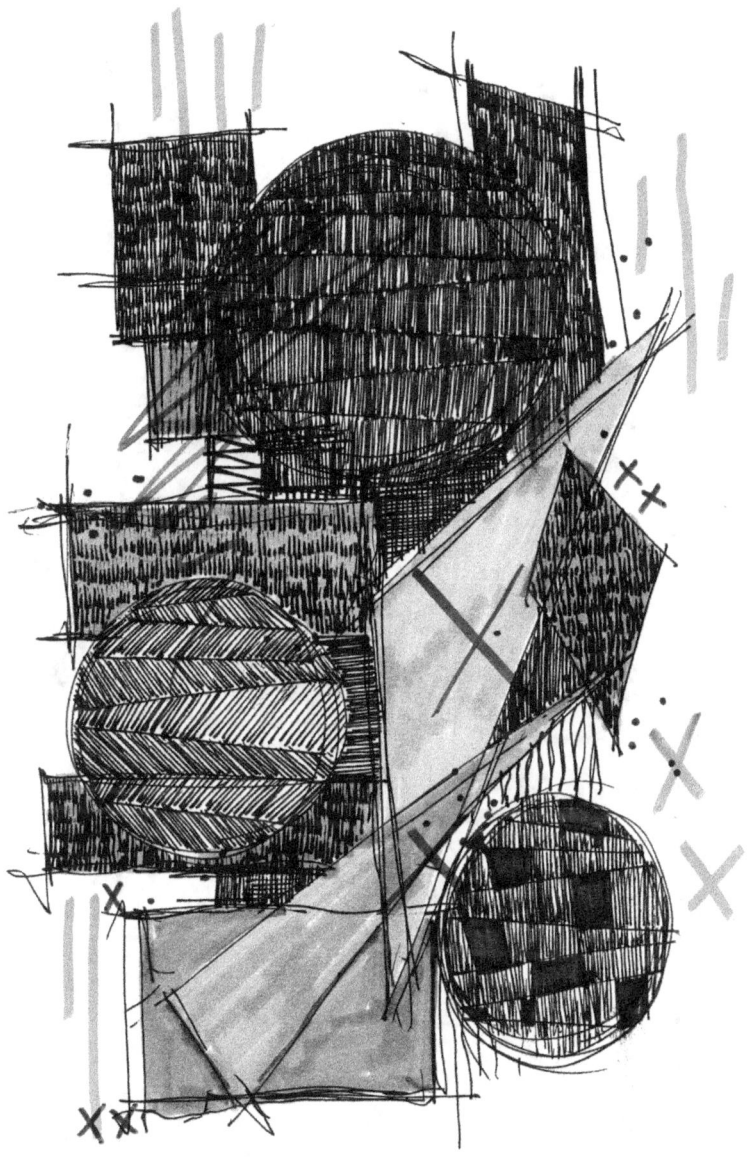

Dana Krystle

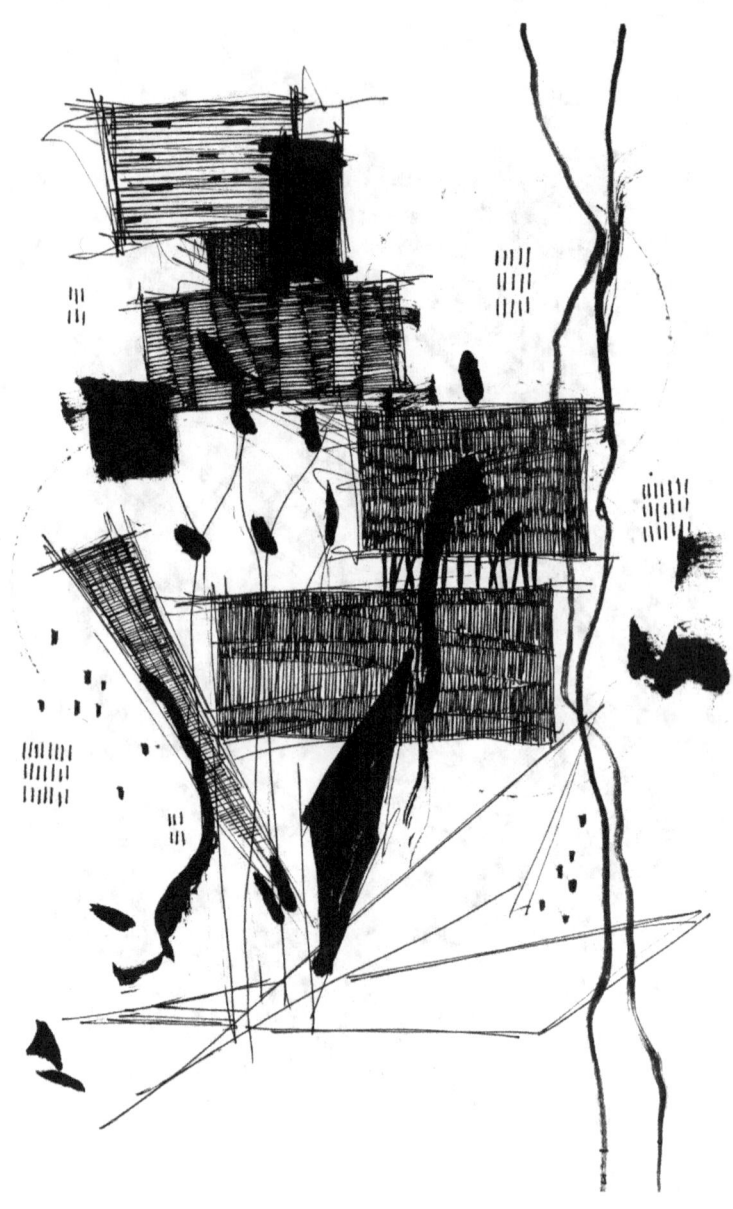

The Monochrome Collection Vol.1

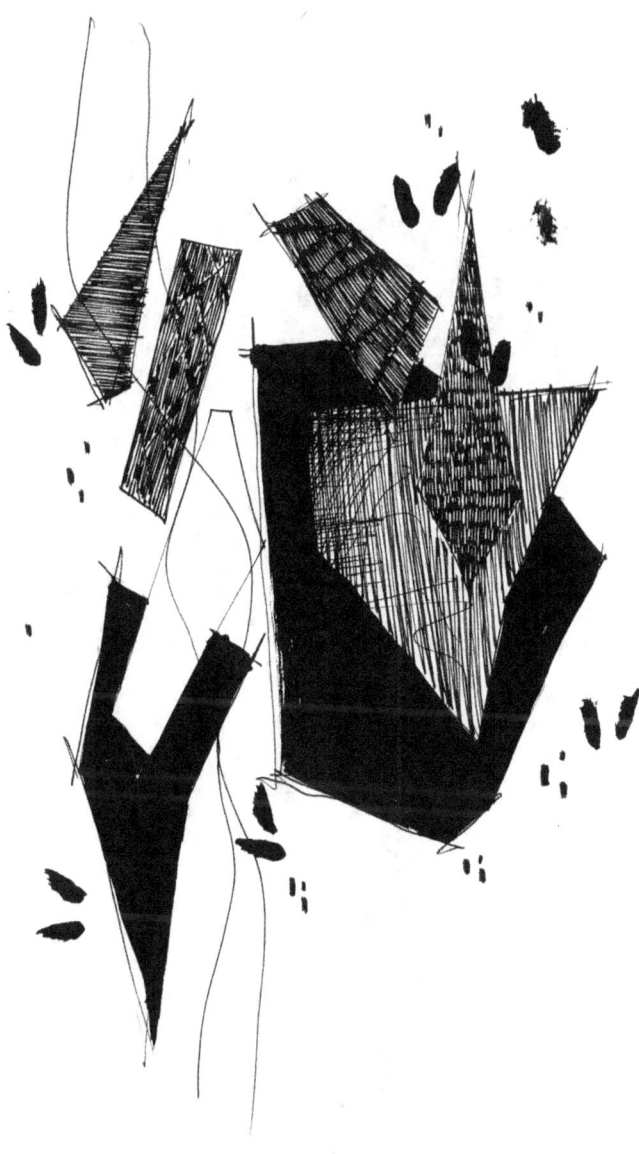

Dana Krystle

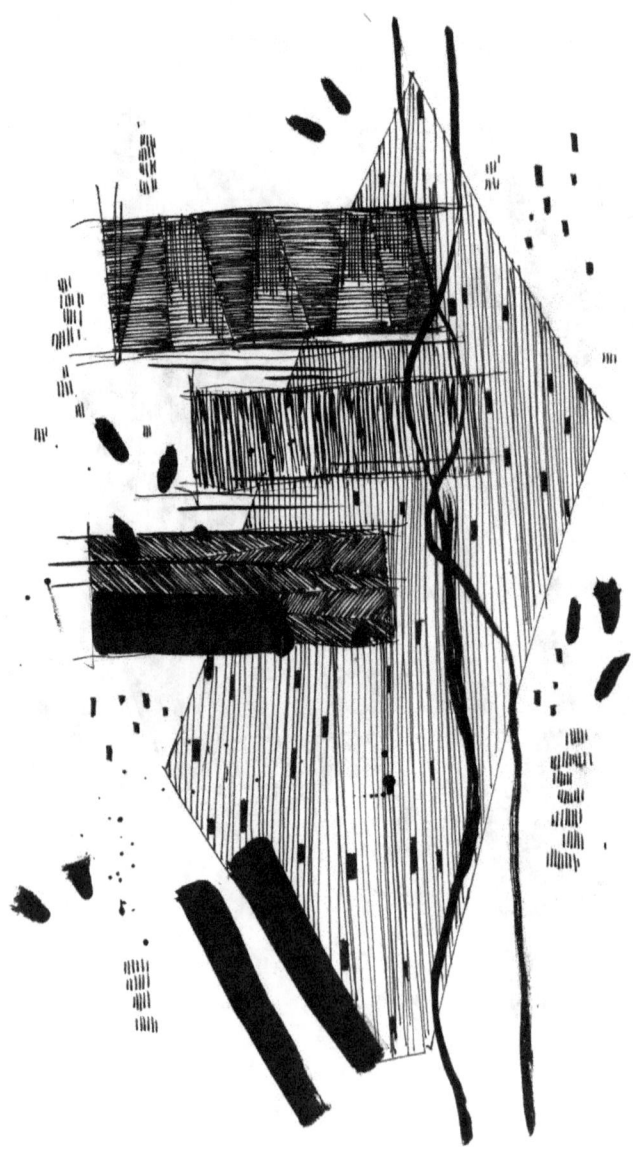

The Monochrome Collection Vol.1

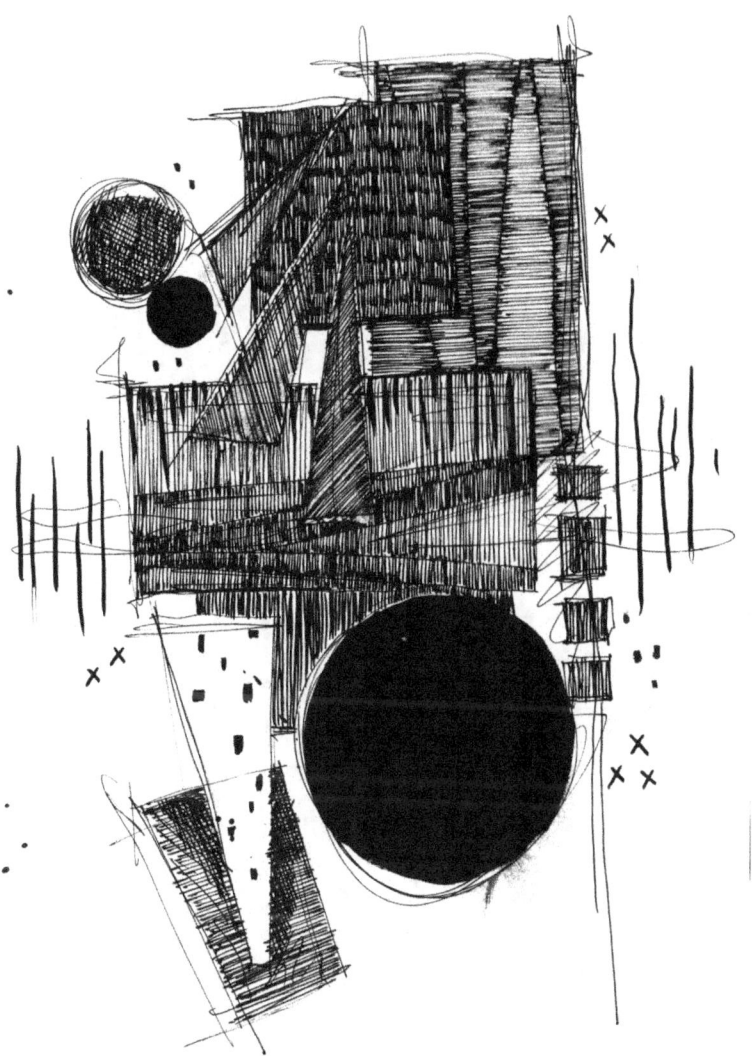

Also by Dana Krystle

Pretentious Butterflies | Poetry Book
Book of Fragments | Art Book
Eden in Black | Novel
Sketchbook N°.11 | A series of architecture illustrations
Sketchbook N°.12 | A series of architecture illustrations

www.ingramcontent.com/pod-product-compliance
Lightning Source LLC
Chambersburg PA
CBHW070444220526
45466CB00004B/1766